ROCKHOUNDING
Oregon

**A Guide to the State's
Best Rockhounding Sites**

LARS W. JOHNSON

FALCONGUIDES

GUILFORD, CONNECTICUT
HELENA, MONTANA
AN IMPRINT OF ROWMAN & LITTLEFIELD

FALCONGUIDES®

Copyright © 2014 Rowman & Littlefield

FalconGuides is an imprint of Rowman & Littlefield.
Falcon and FalconGuides are registered trademarks of Rowman & Littlefield.

All photographs by Lars W. Johnson unless otherwise noted.

Distributed by
NATIONAL BOOK NETWORK

Maps: Alena Joy Pearce © Rowman & Littlefield

Library of Congress Cataloging-in-Publication Data

Johnson, Lars W.
Rockhounding Oregon : a guide to the state's best rockhounding sites / Lars W. Johnson.
    pages cm
 Summary: "This book provides detailed directions and GPS coordinates to the best rockhounding sites in Oregon"-- Provided by publisher.
 ISBN 978-0-7627-8366-3 (paperback)
1. Rocks--Collection and preservation--Oregon--Guidebooks. 2. Minerals--Collection and preservation--Oregon--Guidebooks. 3. Fossils--Collection and preservation--Oregon--Guidebooks. 4. Oregon--Guidebooks. I. Title.
 QE445.OyJ64 2014
 552.09795'075--dc23
                                                                    2014015295

Printed in the United States of America

CONTENTS

Overview

ACKNOWLEDGMENTS

This part is like winning a shiny golden award on TV and getting to give my shout-outs. Even though I won't be shuffled off stage by music, I still hope I don't forget anyone who helped to make this dream happen.

My family have always been huge supporters of my dreams and aspirations. I want to start by thanking them first: my mother, Kristi Robinson; my papa, Jerard Johnson; my stepmother, Karen Johnson; my grandmothers Lorraine VanBrocklin and Ardis Johnson; and my little brother, Karl Johnson. Thank you all for your support and for always letting me be who I am.

I want to thank everyone in the Northwest Diehard Rockhounds group especially Chris and Sara Scheckla, Nate and Tammy Macalevy, and Kelly and Jessica Langford; everyone at the Mount Hood Rock Club; my "little sister," Kelley Harmon; Joan Lawhead, at The Fossil Cartel; Laura and Mike Joki, at Rock Your World; Dennis Harnish; KT Meyers; Judy Elkins; Jessica Shenk and Chris Rose, at The Spectrum Sunstone Mine; Ryan Coggins, for his years of friendship and Internet access; Robin, Steve, and Chris Haun, for getting me out of a couple sticky situations; Aiden of Nyssa for the ride and water; Bare Bones Bar in Portland for being my virtual office and always having a cold one waiting for me after a long rockhounding trip; Les Schwab Tires; and the music of the Melvins and Big Business for keeping me sane and awake while driving night and day, all over Oregon researching this book.

Last, but certainly not least, I want to give my deepest thanks to my lovely, talented, and stunningly beautiful best friend, Sally Franklin. She is truly the most precious gem I have ever found in this great state of Oregon. I absolutely could not have done this book without her love and continuous support. From making gourmet meals in the field, to finding rocks I wasn't, to editing and critiquing my work, her assistance with making this book happen was unsurpassable. I cherish you, number one.

INTRODUCTION

Writing this guidebook was a dream come true. Rockhounding is my absolute favorite pastime, bordering on obsession, and having the opportunity to share my passion with others is a complete honor. Following the footsteps of past guidebook authors and discovering my own sites was an experience I will never forget.

I believe rockhounds should share their knowledge. Keeping each other informed and updated about old and new sites is vital if we want our hobby to continue to be exciting and rewarding. Remember, most of these sites are on *public* land, and we should all have an opportunity to enjoy our great mineral-rich lands. We are rockhounds after all, not gold miners, and we should always be willing to share our experiences and collecting localities with other rock-hounds. You don't necessarily have to hold someone's hand and lead them to a pit, but some directions on a map and some suggestive guidance can really encourage the rockhounding spirit. Share what you find and you will be rewarded with the same.

I personally visited and collected at every site in this book. I might give Haystack Rock a half credit, as I kept trying to explore off-road and got myself high centered twice. Even though hiking out and rescue missions occupied most of my time at Haystack Rock, I did manage to find lots of good material on my hike out.

While researching this book I put in a lot of numbers. I drove more than 25,000 miles of Oregon roads; visited more than 135 potential collecting locations; saw all thirty-six Oregon counties; collected just under one metric ton of material; crossed the 45th Parallel nearly sixty times; took more than 250 GPS waypoints; took thousands of photos; flattened ten tires, four of which were completely blown; got stuck in mud/snow/loose gravel four times and high centered twice; drank sixteen milk shakes; got bit by three ticks; and stayed in thirteen flea-bag motels and five nice hotels without bringing home one bedbug. All of these things, good and bad, added up to one of the most amazing adventures of my life.

This book can be used in many ways. First and foremost, you can use the sites to plan the ultimate Oregon rockhounding adventure. Some people, myself included, use guidebooks like this as a personal checklist. I write notes all over my books; I add my own GPS coordinates, correct typos of mileage, and any information I may need to remember about a particular site or material. I hope you do the same with this book and use it as a tool to expand your own knowledge of Oregon. If you are using this material on an electronic device, such as a tablet, be sure to add lots of electronic notes.

OREGON'S GEOLOGY

The boundless land now known as Oregon was once a fierce and volatile place. Although it must have been an amazing spectacle of geologic fireworks, it was no place for a simple rockhound or any human being for that matter. Millions upon millions of years of violent earthquakes, explosive volcanos, and floods of biblical proportion shaped the land we know today. The state can be divided into separate geological provinces based on how and when each area was formed and the rocks you find in them. The most important events are in chronological order as follows.

The Blue Mountains are formed of exotic terranes that began forming around 400–170 million years ago underwater when the Pacific Ocean's waves were crashing upon what currently is Idaho. Volcanic island arcs, much like Hawaii, eventually attached with North America as they moved westward. Fossils found in these mountains prove their offshore beginnings. These rocks are now mostly covered by younger volcanic rocks, such as the Columbia River basalts. Many placer and lode gold deposits have been found in the Blue Mountains.

The Klamath Mountains are similar to the Blue Mountains, forming offshore about 300–100 million years ago and attaching to North America at around 150–100 million years ago. Like the Blues, the Klamaths are made up of highly altered metamorphic and igneous rocks. This area is also known for its large gold deposits.

The Cascade Mountains combines two volcanic mountain ranges in one. The Western Cascades, or Cascade foothills, were formed about 40–10 million years ago. Less than a million years ago, the High Cascades formed creating the iconic peaks we know today. This mountain range contains a considerable amount of fine silicate materials including agates, jaspers, zeolites, and excellent petrified woods.

The Coast Range is about 60–25 million years old and most of it attached itself to North America around 50–30 million years ago. These mountains are made up of igneous rock–producing volcanos surrounded by seafloor sediments and seamounts. These basalts contain many of the famous agates found on Oregon beaches, and many marine fossils can be found in the sediment deposits.

The Willamette Valley was once thought to just be a valley lying between two mountain ranges. Geologists then realized that in the last 10 million years, a lot of powerful volcanism, seismic activity, and massive erosion all helped sculpt this fertile valley. The Portland Basin is currently one of the most seismically active areas in the state. It also has a mountain, Mount Tabor, which has a basketball court in its sunken caldera. Good lapidary material that has weathered out of the Cascades and elsewhere can be found in many creeks and rivers in the Willamette Valley.

The Columbia River Gorge formed approximately 16–6 million years ago in a series of volcanic events originating in Washington and eastern Oregon. Huge amounts of lava covered much of northern Oregon and southern Washington, some reaching all the way to the ocean. Many of these lava flows contain great collecting material, but much of it is on private land and difficult to access. Many excellent exposures of this volcanic activity have been carved out by the Columbia River and can be seen along the drive on I-84.

The Basin and Range has been seismically active and moving for the past 15 million years. Some joke that this is the best place in the state to purchase land, because it is slowly but constantly expanding. This area consists mostly of volcanic mountain ranges with intervening basins including the Alvord Desert. These mountains and basins are rich in mineral deposits and this province alone could keep a rockhound busy for life. This area also has many excellent hot springs, or rockhound bathtubs.

The Owyhee Upland found in the southeastern corner of Oregon was formed by volcanic activity around 15–10 million years ago, and there has even been activity as recently as 1 million years ago. This volcanically formed area is rich in excellent collectable lapidary material. This is yet another region that a rockhound could spend a lifetime in.

The Deschutes Basin is composed of ash, stream sediments, and Cascade lavas that began collecting around 7–4 million years ago. They now form a sort of volcanic layer cake. These deposits are rich in minerals, but due to lack of public land are difficult to gain access to.

The High Lava Plains were formed by some of the most recent rhyolite and basalt eruptions in Oregon. These events began in eastern Oregon and continued west to near Bend. The Newberry Volcano erupted only 1,200 years ago. This province offers many excellent rockhounding opportunities such as Little Glass Butte and its huge obsidian flow.

Oregon's geology is as diverse as its mineral collecting opportunities. The scenic landscape of the state will have you in awe during your travels. At times while collecting, you may find it difficult to decide where to look: at the rocks on the ground or the picturesque scenery around you. Be sure to bring a camera for it all. Many geological markers are found at highway pullouts around the state. Keep your eyes peeled for these little gems of information.

OREGON ROCKHOUNDING

It's been said that Oregon is where rockhounds go to die. From agates to zeolites, the Beaver State's mineral-rich geology offers enough rockhounding opportunities that it certainly feels like heaven. With access to abundant public lands and many top-notch fee-dig operations, you will find no shortage of opportunities for mineral and fossil collecting in Oregon. Every corner of the state seems to be bursting at the seams with collectable minerals. According to the book, *Agates: Treasures of the Earth*, "Oregon has yielded more different kinds of agates than any other place in the world." From sunstones in the high desert sagebrush, to agates at the rocky coast, to augite in the pine-covered mountains, Oregon offers as many different minerals as it does ecosystems to collect them in.

Stunning vistas, exquisite scenery, and remarkable landscapes serve as great complements to rockhounding in Oregon. Your travels may also lead you to an appreciation of Oregon history. The state historical society has many informational markers; take the time to stop and read. Past railroad, fishing, lumber, and mining initiatives, as well as the influx of emigrants along the Oregon and Applegate Trails, are still affecting the character of Oregon's landscape, people, and towns.

Oregonians have been longtime rockhounds. Oregon had its own gold rush in the mid 1800s, attracting swarms of optimistic miners to the region. Many of the state's agate beds were discovered around this time, and the material was soon being shipped to cutting centers around the world. The famous opal thundereggs from Opal Butte were reportedly first discovered by a shepherd in the late 1800s. By the 1920s, Oregon opal was all the rage in New York; Tiffany & Company made exquisite, fine jewelry with it and began setting trends with the unique material. Unfortunately the Opal Butte deposit is now claimed and public collecting is not allowed. Fortunately there are many other opal collecting opportunities in Oregon. The United States' very first rock club, The Oregon Agate and Mineral Society, was started in Portland in 1933 and is still very active.

Participating in a rock club can be an excellent way to learn more about the hobby, to work with hard-to-get lapidary equipment, and to meet a lot of other people with rocks in their heads. Joining a rock club can also be a great way to gain access to lands that are not generally open to rockhounds. From time to time some of the rock clubs in and around the greater Portland metro area are allowed access to Clear Creek in Vernonia—on private property, normally closed to individuals, and known for its colorful carnelian. There are also many rockhounding groups and forums on the Internet. Forums such as the ones found at rockhoundstation1.net and pebblepup.com offer an arena for people to talk about their favorite subject, rocks. Social media sites such as Facebook also have many groups dedicated to the hobby and even some dedicated to a particular material. I belong to a group on Facebook called Northwest Diehard Rockhounds and have met and dug with many of its very active and involved members. Even with decades of organized and unorganized rock collecting, Oregon still offers many productive and enjoyable rockhounding opportunities for all.

There are many rockhounding opportunities in Oregon that are only available at certain times of year. For instance during the Madras Pow-Wow, an excellent rock show that usually happens the weekend before the 4th of July, some of the local ranches open their gates and highly prized material to rockhounds. The participating ranches may vary from year to year, but can include popular collecting sites such as Friends Ranch (thundereggs, agate, and petrified wood), Marston Ranch (jasper and agate), McDonald Ranch (petrified wood, agate, and jasp-agate), Ochs Ranch (thundereggs), and Nartz Ranch (agate). Expect to pay a small fee per vehicle and a per pound fee for material. Material from these ranches sells for much more once removed and put into a rock shop.

Another way to find otherwise inaccessible rockhounding spots or just to have someone show you what to do is to hire a guide. High Desert Gems and Minerals (owners of the Spectrum Sunstone Mine) offer a trip that takes you to their sunstone mine and other claims they hold on the west coast. Jason Hinkle of www.oregonthundereggs.com offers guided trips to his thunderegg claim in the Ochoco Mountains. Do a search on the Internet for more guided tour possibilities.

ROCKHOUNDING BASICS

Before embarking on any rockhounding adventure, there are a few basic rules that every rockhound should know and follow. Oregon has a wealth of gems, minerals, and fossils that with proper protection and regulations will hopefully be there for generations to enjoy.

OFFICIALLY OREGON

State Rock—Thunderegg
Thundereggs are a spherical nodular mass of rhyolitic material containing an interior of agate, jasper, opal, and/or other minerals. The thunderegg was designated the Oregon state rock in 1965. Thundereggs can be dug at Richardson's Rock Ranch, Lucky Strike Mine, White Fir, White Rock, Whistler Springs, Crane Creek, Succor Creek, and McDermitt.

State Gemstone—Sunstone
Oregon sunstones are a variety of orthoclase feldspar with copper inclusions that make our state gem so unique. They were designated as such in 1987. The Bureau of Land Management (BLM) has set aside ten acres for public rockhounding use and many fee-dig mines offer collection opportunities in the Rabbit Basin near Plush, Oregon. There are more sunstone deposits in Harney County, but the mines are not open to the public.

State Twin Minerals—Josephinite and Oregonite
Both are nickel-iron minerals believed to have come from deep within the Earth's lower mantle. They were designated the Oregon State Twin Minerals in 2013. Josephinite and Oregonite can be found in Josephine Creek, Josephine County, Oregon.

State Fossil—Metasequoia
Metasequoia, or Dawn Redwood, once flourished in North America during the Miocene Age and subsequently left its fossil imprints all over Oregon. First described as a fossil in 1941, the tree was believed to be extinct. Shortly thereafter in 1944, it was "rediscovered" in China. Metasequoia fossils can be dug in Fossil, Oregon. Metasequoia was designated the Oregon State Fossil in 2005.

COLLECTING REGULATIONS
Minerals
The BLM and USDA Forest Service (USFS) consider rockhounding an outdoor recreation. Just like fishing and other outdoor activities approved on public lands, rockhounding is not without its rules and regulations. Recreational noncommercial collecting is only allowed using hand tools. If

people were allowed to bring mechanized tools into public collecting areas, there wouldn't be much left for future generations of mineral collectors. As much as I would love to bring a jackhammer to many hard-rock digging sites, I completely respect the ideals of both hard work and leaving something for the next person.

There are a few rockhounding sites located on public lands that are close to Wilderness Study Areas or Wilderness Areas. While on BLM land you are allowed to dig holes. When on wilderness land, rockhounding is limited to surface collection only, with digging off limits. White Rock is a good example of such a site. The old White Rock thunderegg beds now lie in wilderness land and digging in them is not allowed anymore. Fortunately there are lots of thunderegg beds on the side of the fence you can legally dig in. The use of mechanized or motorized travel on wilderness land is prohibited as well.

In 2012, the BLM put restrictions on beach agate collecting, limiting all beach collecting to a one-gallon bucket full, per day, but not to exceed three gallons per year.

Petrified Wood

The collection of petrified wood is allowed on public land. A federal law passed in 1962 states that rockhounds are limited to collecting twenty-five pounds plus one piece per day, but not to exceed 250 pounds per person per year. People may not pool their limits together to obtain pieces weighing over 250 pounds. The removal of petrified wood weighing over 250 pounds may only be done with a permit.

Fossils

Common invertebrate and plant fossils (such as snail, clam, and leaf fossils) may be collected on public lands for noncommercial personal use. The collection of any vertebrate fossils or other paleontological resources is prohibited without a permit. Paleontological Resources Preservation under the Omnibus Public Lands Act of 2009 defines a paleontological resource as: any fossilized remains, traces, or imprints of organisms, preserved in or on the Earth's crust that are of paleontological interest and provide information about the history of life on Earth. A paleontological resource permit is required to collect paleontological resources of scientific interest. Anything collected with a permit will remain the property of the United States and will be preserved for the public for scientific research and education.

Artifacts

All historic and prehistoric remains on public land are protected by law. This includes, but is not limited to arrowheads, points, feathers, whole or broken pots, stone tools, basketry, or even old bottles. Artifacts were first protected under the Preservation of American Antiquities Act of 1906. The Federal Land Policy and Management Act of 1976 and the Archaeological Resources Protection Act of 1979 later added even more laws protecting these artifacts. The excavation, destruction, vandalism, or removal of archaeological resources (historic and prehistoric) from public lands is punishable by law.

TOOLS AND SUPPLIES

The most important tool you will use on every rockhounding trip is your brain. Be safe, be smart, be aware, and be very prepared. Be safe, and know your physical limits before traversing the terrain. Be aware of your surroundings and any obstacles they may contain, whether crumbling terrain, fast river currents, or any potentially dangerous local flora and fauna, such as poison oak or rattlesnakes. There's an area in Washington nicknamed "Dead Rockhound Gulch." Many people have died there over the years because they were not using common sense. They collected in an unsafe area and paid the ultimate price, just to collect quartz crystals. No rock is ever worth losing your life over. Use good judgment when collecting at any site.

Now that the serious part is over, let's get to the fun stuff: tools!

Like my papa always says, you need the right tool for the job. As a hardware store owner, he knows a thing or two about the subject. Rockhounding is no exception! Be prepared for the task at hand. To begin, there is a huge difference between a rock hammer and a carpenter's hammer. Rock hammers and geology picks are tempered to withstand repeated heavy blows to hard rock. Carpenter's hammers are designed for nails and can easily splinter or break, causing serious bodily injury when used on rocks. Do not use them for rockhounding at any cost. The best rock hammers and picks are made from a solid piece of steel, versus hammers with the head and neck being composed of different materials. My personal favorite rock hammers are made by Estwing. Rockhounds and masons have trusted this brand's durability and design for decades.

Geology picks are probably the most useful and recognizable tool of the rockhound. With one blunt end and the other pointed, a geology pick can be used to hammer, pick, and pry material out of the ground or host rock. They can come in many lengths and weights. Find which size works best for you. Being 6'4", I like the E3-23LP by Estwing, as the handle is a bit longer than the others.

The next tool most used by rockhounds is a sledgehammer. They are used to bust open rock and to pound chisels and gads into cracks in host rock. Sledgehammers start at three pounds and work their way up to sixteen pounds. As you did when choosing a geology pick, find the size and weight of sledgehammer that works best for your needs.

For breaking up large pieces of rock, such as basalt, and exposing pockets of minerals within, chisels, gads, star drills, wedges, and pry bars are essential. Chisels are hand tools with a flat end; gads are the same, but with a pointed end; star drills have a star-shaped end. All are struck with a hammer or sledge to split the rock open. Miners digging geodes at Walker Valley in Washington have come up with some ingenious wedges used for cleaving large pieces of basalt. Truck springs have been cut and filed into a wedge shape. They call these basalt splitters "Walker Valley Wedges." If you can get your hands on one or make some, I'm sure they'd be great Oregon wedges too. Pry bars are used to move material or pop it out of the host rock. They can range from a foot and a half to several feet in length. Paint scrapers are used to split and expose layers of shale when hunting for fossils.

If digging is the chosen method of attack at the site, an array of shovels and trowels are necessary. Both spade and flathead shovels are useful depending on the site. Small folding shovel and garden trowels are good excavators when working in tight spaces.

Large picks or pickaxes are also other essential tools needed when digging a large hole. They tear up tough dirt and make shoveling it out a heck of a lot easier. Estwing makes a fantastic pick called the Paleo Pick. Common mining picks and awls work great too.

Always wear eye protection when wielding tools. Protect your hands with a well-fitting pair of gloves and consider wearing a handkerchief over your face when dust or flying rock chips are present. Screens are useful for the collection of sunstones and some smaller material at sites such as Hampton Butte. You can find them in some rock shops, prospecting stores, and online. I prefer to make my own and have a collection of screens in various sizes for various purposes.

Spray bottles, a bucket of water, and an old toothbrush or nail brush are great to have around for washing off stubbornly sticky dirt to better judge material. Wetting down some minerals, especially silicates such as agate and jasper, can also give you an idea of what it will look like when it is polished.

Something to carry and store the treasures you find is very important as well. Fossils need special consideration; initially wrapping them in paper towels or newspaper will protect them on the trip home, as much of the material is rather fragile. Keep a box of freezer bags and a permanent marker with your supplies. The bags are great for storing your smaller finds and to keep material from different sites separated. The marker comes in handy for labeling. Sometimes after a long rockhounding trip you can forget what rocks came from which site. A small bucket, backpack, or shoulder bag is fine when collecting beach agates and other small float material. When the material starts to get big, the tried and true classic way to carry and store minerals is the plastic five-gallon bucket. A lot of rockhounds have a huge number of five-gallon buckets sitting around filled with material, and I am no exception. I'm constantly on the hunt for more buckets; I never seem to have enough. There is now a golf-style caddie with wheels that holds a five-gallon bucket. Another good method for carrying heavy rocks is a sturdy metal frame backpack. Tony Funk of idahorockshop.com swears by this method. He says he's getting too old to lug around five-gallon buckets full of rocks and I'm beginning to agree with him.

TOP TEN OREGON ROCKHOUNDING SITES

This is my personal top-ten list for Oregon, places I continue to visit year after year and never seem to tire of collecting at. They are also places a person can go for the first time and find success. In no particular order I present to you my list:

Rabbit Basin for sunstones
Short Beach for agate, jasper, and zeolites
Hampton Butte for green petrified wood
Rome for snakeskin agates
Richardson's Rock Ranch for thundereggs
Graveyard Point for agate
Congleton Hollow/Dendrite Butte for agate limb casts
Glass Buttes for obsidian
The town of Fossil, for fossil leaves
McDermitt for petrified wood, agate, jasper, and thundereggs

HOW TO USE THIS BOOK

Land type: A brief description of the terrain you can expect to be in at the digging site. West of the Cascades is mostly forested. East of the Cascades is mostly sagebrush with some pockets of forest.

County: What county the digging site is in.

GPS: Lists the GPS coordinates of the particular site or sites. I used a Garmin Legend ETrex for all the readings in the book. My readings were done in WGS84 standard and I used *National Geographic Oregon Topo* software to confirm all GPS data. Google Earth can also be a good resource for researching the terrain of a site you intend on visiting.

Best season: The weather can ultimately determine the outcome of any rockhounding trip. One thing for certain in Oregon is that it is going to rain. Even in the summer, it rains. While rain and storms make for great beach collecting, it turns eastern Oregon roads into a nasty gumbo that even the best 4WD vehicles can get stuck in. Always check weather reports before heading out on any rockhounding trip. No matter what the weatherman predicts, be prepared for any type of weather. It's been said that if you don't like the weather in Oregon, wait ten minutes. Conditions can change quickly.

Different times of the year lend themselves to different types of rockhounding. For instance late summer is best for river and creek collecting as the water is low, exposing more gravel bars. Knowing when to be in a particular area greatly increases your chances of finding material.

Land manager: It's very important to know what land you're planning to collect on. Always check with the land manager for the status of each site before you visit. Collecting rules, regulations, and land access are always subject to change. Contact the land manager before dedicating a long drive to a site that may have changed hands or may be unexpectedly inaccessible due to snow, rain, landslides, wildfires, etc. Most of the sites in this book are on accessible public land. A handful of sites are found on private land. Some of the private land sites are fee-dig operations that have set days and hours. Others are found on private land where the owner has allowed rockhounds to casually collect over the years. Sites like these should be treated with the utmost respect. Keep your collecting small. Any giant digging operations or holes/garbage left behind are great ways to get a site shut down to everybody. If you visit a site and find that the owner has changed his or her mind and erected fences and/or signs, respect their property rights and stay out.

Material: This section lists what types of rocks and minerals you can expect to find when visiting the site. Material is generally listed from most to least abundant. More detailed descriptions will be found in the rockhounding section of each site.

Tools: This section will list the tools you will need to bring for success. Sometime many tools are listed for a site, depending on what you're looking to remove. I never go out without being armed with a plethora of tools and accessories for those just-in-case moments. When exploring you can run into material you need a completely different set of tools to collect. I've often found myself in the middle of the high desert, wishing for a tool I left at home in the basement. On that note, I have also made it home realizing I left my favorite pick 400 miles away in the high desert. I now spray-paint some of my tools bright with fluorescent colors to make them noticeable in the dirt, reminding me to pick them up.

Vehicle: Recommends the type of vehicle you will need to gain access to a site. Some places you can bring a minivan packed with the whole family, while in others you absolutely need high-clearance 4WD to get anywhere near the site. Don't exaggerate your vehicle's capabilities. Be fully practiced in driving your vehicle both forward and backward. Oregon has some very remote collecting sites where you don't want to get stuck because you decided to push the limits with your vehicle.

Accommodations: Lists the closest general camping, RV parks, and cities with hotels/motels. Most sites open for collecting are on BLM land, which is generally open for primitive camping. There's a spot on the south side of Little Glass Butte that I absolutely love. I spent my 29th birthday rockhounding from this lovely campsite. We even had a salmon dinner cooked on the fire and a birthday banana-crème pie with candles and all the trimmings. The accommodations may be primitive, but the dining can be fine. Many sites also have more modern camping facilities available. Several FalconGuides as well as many other print publications and online forums are dedicated to Oregon and can be great resources for finding that perfect spot to stay.

Special attractions: Listed are mostly sites of geologic, scenic, or historic interest, including nearby hot springs. There's nothing better than being able to take a hot bath and soak your achy bones after digging in the dirt all day. Take some time to stop at vistas, points of interest, and historical markers. You never know what you're going to find or what you may learn. Sally Franklin and I had an unexpected blast stopping at the Jean Baptiste

Charbonneau Gravesite near Rome. Bringing along guidebooks such as *Hiking Hot Springs in the Pacific Northwest* and *Roadside Geology of Oregon* can help you find other fantastic places to visit and give you a better knowledge of the state as you travel.

Finding the site: In this section you will find detailed directions to the digging sites in an area. My mileage was taken in my trusty, often dusty, 2006 Toyota Tacoma (aka Fat Girl), but all odometers seem to be just a little different, so take tenths of a mile with a grain of salt. I tried to list all mileposts, mines, signs, and other pertinent landmarks to help you find the way. Remember that roads are always subject to change and/or closure. Always check with the land manager for current road status. Signs can sometimes be hidden by vegetation, stolen, damaged, worn, in disrepair, or vandalized to the point you could use the sign itself to screen rocks. I've noticed people seem to love to shoot signs out in the middle of nowhere.

Rockhounding: This section goes into more detail about what you can expect to find at a particular site, how to dig it, and anything else you should know about a site or the area you're in. Though not a focus, any recommendations for nearby gold panning may also be found in this section. With the exception of Juniper Ridge, I personally visited every site in the book. I tried to keep information as up to date as possible, but as with any other resource, everything is subject to change. Again, always check with the land manager on the status of any site.

Map Legend

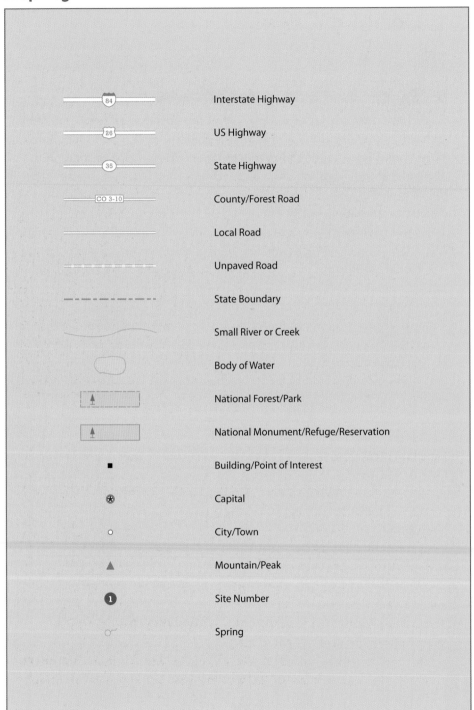

84	Interstate Highway
26	US Highway
35	State Highway
CO 3-10	County/Forest Road
	Local Road
	Unpaved Road
	State Boundary
	Small River or Creek
	Body of Water
	National Forest/Park
	National Monument/Refuge/Reservation
■	Building/Point of Interest
✪	Capital
○	City/Town
▲	Mountain/Peak
❶	Site Number
⚲	Spring

1. Beneke Creek

A partially exposed 4-inch concretion in the quarry wall. Bring your hard-rock tools to break them free.

Land type: Forested quarry
County: Clatsop
GPS: A: N46 00.418' / W123 30.425', 1,013 ft. (quarry); B: N46 00.640' / W123 30.933', 1,011 ft. (Beneke Creek)
Best season: Late spring–fall
Land manager: ODF—Clatsop State Forest
Material: Fossil concretions
Tools: Geology pick, hammer, chisel, gad
Vehicle: 4WD suggested
Accommodations: Primitive camping throughout Clatsop State Forest
Special attraction: Banks-Vernonia Trail
Finding the site: From Portland take US 26 to Buxton and then head north on OR 47 to Vernonia. From here take OR 202 west to Jewell. Just west of town turn right

Tillamook State Forest

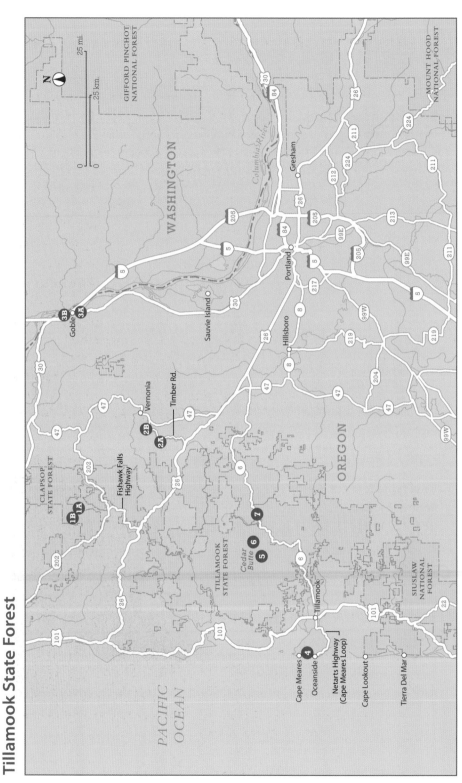

onto Beneke Creek Road. Travel about 5.2 miles to a fork in the road. To the right is Site A and to the left Site B. Site A is reached by driving 0.7 mile to another fork, at which you will keep left. The quarry is about 0.1 mile up this road, with an open area to park. The GPS marking for this site is just northwest of the parking area, below the road cutting through the quarry. Site B is reached by taking the first fork of Beneke Creek Road to the left and driving about 1.2 miles to a small bridge crossing Beneke Creek. Park at the bridge where I made my GPS reading and search up- and downstream in the creek from here.

Rockhounding

This area's marine fossils and concretions have attracted fossil collectors for many years. Unfortunately many of those sites are now inaccessible, not producing much, or illegal to collect at. The police patrol some well-known areas and are not shy about handing out tickets. Fortunately the two sites listed here are legal and productive places to find concretions. (Nearby Buster Creek Quarry is known for agate and zeolites, but every time I have visited, it is being actively worked and the workers are never happy to see me.)

Site A is located in the old Jewell Quarry. The walls of the quarry contain the concretions. Look for the round balls in the bedrock and for those that have weathered out and rolled down the hill. Some of the concretions found in the bedrock are easier to remove than others. Bring your hard-rock mining tools to help with the stubborn ones.

A view of the concretion-bearing quarry wall at Site A. There are some good ones through those bushes.

Site B is Beneke Creek. Search up and down this generally shallow creek for concretions. This is a good place to collect a lot of concretions as you don't have to work them out of bedrock. Bring your mucking boots/shoes and a sturdy collecting bag.

Fossils found in concretions are hit or miss. I never have much luck with them, but have seen great examples from this area found by other rockhounds. Gather as many as you can to increase your odds of finding a fossil inside. Fossils found in the concretions can include but are not limited to crabs, shark teeth, and snails, but most of the time they will be empty. The concretions can range in size from a plum to a cantaloupe. The bigger ones are usually empty.

Every rockhound seems to have a different way of opening concretions. Some prefer to just whack away with a hammer and test their luck in splitting them. I've also heard of people soaking the concretions, freezing them, and waiting for them to split. Any which way you choose to crack it open, you'll probably have to do some gluing when you're done. It's also a good idea to use a product such as PaleoBOND to coat the exposed fossil to keep it from disintegrating.

2. Nehalem River

An excellent specimen of Vernonia area carnelian. Rice Northwest Museum of Rocks and Minerals specimen

See map on page 16.
Land type: Forested riverbank
County: Columbia
GPS: A: N45 48.898' / W123 16.876', 679 ft. (bridge); B: N45 50.973' / W123 14.503',
643 ft. (Airport Park)
Best season: Summer
Land manager: BLM—Salem
Material: Jasper, agate, carnelian, petrified wood, fossil concretions
Tools: Geology pick, collecting bag
Vehicle: Any
Accommodations: Developed and primitive camping along Nehalem River
Special attraction: Banks-Vernonia Trail
Finding the site: From US 26, drive to Timber Junction. Take NW Vernonia Road
north which will eventually turn into Timber Road. Keep an eye out for the river,

gravel bars, and potential places to pull out and park. Site A is found about 5.7 miles down the road. Pull out and park at the bridge that crosses the river. To reach site B continue north on Timber Road 3.5 miles and then turn left onto Airport Road. Keep left at the fork, pay the modest day fee, and find a place to park near the river.

Rockhounding

The Nehalem River and Clear Creek have been long known for their agate and highly prized carnelian, but there is very limited access to the Nehalem and Clear Creek is off limits due to private timber land and fish habitat. Some local rock clubs get special permission from the timber company to collect around Clear Creek from time to time, another reason why joining a rock club can be so beneficial.

The GPS listings are two places one can find legal easy to moderate access to the river. Site A is a bridge crossing the Nehalem. Access at the bridge is iffy at best. The climb down can be a bit precarious. I found an easier way in about 0.1 mile north of the bridge. Use caution walking the road especially with kids and pets, as it is frequented by log trucks. Airport Park (Site B) is a day use fee area, but provides good gravel bar access and has camping, picnic tables, big toys, and an outhouse. Check out other campgrounds in the area that may provide river access.

Search the Nehalem River for good gravel exposures. Watch for crayfish that look like carnelian.

Agate and jasper are the most common finds. The agate tends to be clear with some banding and the jasper is mostly red to yellow. Keep your eyes peeled for elusive bright red/orange carnelian. The carnelian found in the area is top notch, but you'll be very lucky to find some. Fossil-bearing concretions can be found throughout the area as well. You can even see them poking out of sandstone outcrops along the roads near the river. Low-grade petrified wood can be obtained as well.

The Nehalem River is notorious for flooding. While this wreaks havoc on the neighboring communities, it does stir up the river gravels, exposing fresh material for rockhounds. The river is also home to lots of crayfish. While they can trick you into thinking you're seeing a nice piece of carnelian, they do make for good eats.

3. Goble

Cubic chabazite and apophyllite on basalt, from the Goble area.
RICE NORTHWEST MUSEUM OF ROCKS AND MINERALS SPECIMEN

See map on page 16.

Land type: Forested basalt outcrops; rock piles

County: Columbia

GPS: A: N46 00.463' / W122 52.538', 27 ft.; B: N46 01.220' / W122 52.739', 63 ft.

Best season: Any

Land manager: Oregon Parks and Recreation

Material: Zeolites

Tools: Hammer, chisel, gad

Vehicle: Any

Accommodations: None on site—motels and RV parks in area

Special attraction: Sauvie Island

Finding the site: Traveling from Portland or Astoria use US 30 and head toward Goble. Site A is a pile of rocks found just off the highway at Jaquish Road. To reach site B continue north along US 30 0.8 mile to Neer City Road on your left. Take this road and head less than 0.1 mile up the hill to a small pullout on the left at the end of the guardrail. Park here and find the faint trail leading down the hill to the basalt outcrop under the road. There is a productive quarry farther down Neer City Road, but there were fresh "keep out" signs when I visited in May 2013.

Rockhounding

Many excellent zeolite specimens have been found over the years in the basalt surrounding the Goble area. It is the type locality for tschernichite, a zeolite named after former Rice Museum curator and author of *Zeolites of the World*, Rudy Tschernich. Other members of the zeolite family that can be found here include but are not limited to chabazite, stilbite, and thomsonite. The Northwest Rice Museum in Hillsboro has a wonderful display of zeolites, many from Oregon, which all rockhounds should check out.

Heavy hammers, gads, and chisels are just about the only way you're going to find and recover material from these sites. Some tougher crystals can be retrieved from the soil, but specimens in matrix tend to be much more aesthetically pleasing. Be prepared to split open a lot of basalt to expose fresh zeolite-filled amygdules. Look for boulders and exposures with larger exposed pockets. Large pockets contain large minerals.

Eye protection and gloves are essential if you plan on swinging a hammer here. The host basalt is very hard and likes to shoot out when you break it. It always seems to have an especially good aim for your face. If you have small children or pets, be on the lookout if you plan on collecting at Site A near the highway.

The pile of zeolite-bearing basalt found at Site A in Goble. Bring a good hammer.

4. Short Beach

A small sample of chalcedony, agates, and jaspers found at Short Beach.

See map on page 16.

Land type: Ocean beach

County: Tillamook

GPS: N45 28.370' / W123 58.131', 109 ft.

Best season: Winter–late spring

Land manager: BLM

Material: Agate, jasper, calcite, zeolites, quartz, petrified wood

Tools: Geology pick, hammer, gem scoop

Vehicle: Any

Accommodations: Camping along US 101; lodging in Tillamook

Special attractions: Cape Meares Lighthouse; Pacific Coast Scenic Byway

Finding the site: From US 101 in Tillamook, take OR 131 W/ 3rd Street and follow it about 8.8 miles to Cape Meares Loop where you will take a slight right up the hill. Drive 1.2 miles until you see the ocean and a small parking area near a fence to your right. The GPS reading marks the trail leading down to the beach. This site can also be reached by taking Bayshore Drive from OR 131.

Rockhounding

Collecting here, like most Oregon coast beach locations, is just a matter of walking around and picking up rocks. Get to the beach just after high tide and start collecting as the surf heads out. It's easier to find material when the gravel is wet, so don't let a rainy day deter you. A gem scoop is handy for getting things off the ground without straining your back. I also like to use a geology pick for moving rock around to expose fresh material. Great finds can be hidden beneath boring gray rocks.

My good friend Kelley Harmon has led fee rockhounding field trips to this location, which is how I first discovered this wonderful place to collect. For a couple years it was our little secret beach location. Soon enough it was revealed in other guidebooks and the beach seems to be much more popular nowadays. Luckily there's always plenty of material to be had for everyone. Access to this beach is gained only from a long path that is nicely graded with stairs. I'd like to personally thank Roy "The Trail Guy" Wilson for all his hard work installing every step. For more information please visit his website www.shortbeachtrail.org. The hike down to the beach isn't so

A bird's-eye view from the flume at Short Beach. Be careful crossing that creek.

bad, but the walk back up to the parking area with a bucket full of specimens is a different story. If you can't conquer the stairs, try collecting the beaches at nearby Oceanside or Cape Meares.

Abundant agate and jasper can be found the entire stretch of the beach. The agate is mostly small and clear. The occasional carnelian, banded, black, and enhydro agates can also be obtained. Enhydro agates are agates that have bubbles of ancient water trapped inside of them that can be easily seen when backlit. You may see agates still stuck in their basalt host. If it's a large specimen and can be easily separated from its matrix, spend some time carefully extracting it with a geology pick or hammer. Don't waste your time trying to knock out small agates. You'll find plenty of small specimens searching the beach gravels.

Jasper can be found in an array of colors including green, red, yellow, gray, and brown, most of which take a good polish in a tumbler. There's a lot of porous red and green wanna-be jasper lying around too. Look for a waxy luster and conchodial fractures in suspect material. This is a sign of good jasper that will take a polish.

The basalt boulders are also host to many minerals besides agate. Zeolites including heulandite, clinoptillolite, and mordenite are fairly common here, along with the occasional golden calcite rhombs. I once saw a small amethyst geode come off this beach. To obtain zeolites, calcite, or the rare geode, you're going to have to bust open some rock. Search through the small boulders looking for exposed amygdules, hopefully filled in by an array of beautiful minerals. Break open any suspect material to expose fresh pockets. Keep in mind that not all amygdules are created equal. You may have to cleave a lot of rock to find good material. A three- to five-pound rock hammer works best, but if you're good with a geology pick, that will work too. Wear eye protection while hammering away at rocks or near someone who is.

5. Cedar Butte

A small pile of augite crystals at Cedar Butte, with the largest crystal approximately 1 inch.

See map on page 16.

Land type: Forested hillside
County: Tillamook
GPS: N45 35.155' / W123 38.908', 2,208 ft.
Best season: Summer
Land manager: ODF—Tillamook State Forest
Material: Augite
Tools: Geology pick, collecting bag
Vehicle: 4WD suggested
Accommodations: Developed and primitive camping along OR 6
Special attraction: Tillamook Forest Center
Finding the site: On OR 6 (the Wilson River Highway) near milepost 17 you will find a turnoff leading to a bridge that crosses the Wilson River. This is a popular fishing and swimming area. Keep along the gravel road that heads straight up the hill. At about 5.7 miles you will come to a parking area for a trailhead. Just past the parking area is a road leading up the hill to the left. If your rig can make it, take this

A view up the steep hill at Cedar Butte where you will find augite crystals. Careful, it's easy to roll down this one.

road about 0.2 mile to another open parking area where you will park. Look for an overgrown road leading down the hill to your right. Walk this road about 0.3 mile to where the trail makes a hairpin turn. At this point look for an exposed hillside through the woods. That is where you want to go. There are a few paths from here leading through the thicket to the soft dirt of the steep and eroded hillside.

Rockhounding

Cedar Butte provides the rare opportunity to collect augite crystals, a calcium sodium magnesium iron aluminum silicate. Try saying that three times fast. Augite is generally black in color, though some have a slight green tone. The crystals range from about ¼ inch to 1½ inches, most being on the smaller side.

You can easily fill your pockets with nice, yet sometimes pitted, crystals by simply walking around the site and picking them up off the forest floor. Augite is very brittle and many crystals break under light pressure. Try rolling crystals with moderate pressure between your fingers to test their strength and to keep from bringing home material that is just going to fracture and break apart anyway. Strong crystals that aren't as liable to fracture can be tumble polished with the aid of plastic pellets. Crystals can also be found by screening the dirt, but the forest floor in this area stays pretty moist most of the year, so screening could be difficult or impossible.

To get crystals in matrix, you're going to have to work them out of their source, which is easily seen up the very steep hill at the location. Luckily the dirt is soft and most people can easily climb up and use their geology picks to free specimens from the hillside. Children and the elderly should stick to gathering crystals off the ground. Be aware of people below you if you choose to dig uphill. Loose material can pick up speed tumbling down, and so can people. I know from experience. For more geologic information about the Cedar Butte area, please consult *The Ore Bin*, Vol. 31, No. 6 (June 1969).

A few words of caution before you decide to take the drive to the site. The area is heavily worked by timber companies. There are log haulers and trucks carrying large equipment going up and down the mountain. The road is narrow and you can encounter them at any moment. Be confident in your reverse driving as the trucks cannot back up and there are very few places to turn off or around. Give them a wave and a smile as they pass by and maybe they'll tell you if another truck is on its way down. The road can also be very muddy or washed out in spots.

6. Jones Creek

A pitted, yet large agate found in the gravels of Jones Creek. Bring a geology pick to help pry specimens like this out.

See map on page 16.

Land type: Forested creek gravels
County: Tillamook
GPS: N45 35.924' / W123 36.671', 1,406 ft.
Best season: Summer
Land manager: ODF—Tillamook State Forest
Material: Agate, jasper, calcite, pyrite, zeolites
Tools: Geology pick, hammer
Vehicle: Any
Accommodations: Lots of great camping throughout Tillamook State Forest
Special attraction: Tillamook Forest Center
Finding the site: Coming from Portland or Tillamook use OR 6 (NW Wilson River Highway) and travel into the Tillamook State Forest. You will be looking for Jones Creek Road heading north across the river. This road is about 22 miles east of

Tillamook. Continue along Jones Creek Road for 3.0 miles where it will essentially turn into Cedar Creek Road. Jones Creek Road veers off to the right. Continue another 1.2 miles to a pullout on your left.

Rockhounding

Search the gravels of Jones Creek to find agate, jasper, calcite, and pyrite. The agates and jasper are found lying about in the gravel bars. The agate is clear to blue/gray with banding being fairly common. It's mostly tumbler-size material, but large pieces suited for cutting are possible. The jasper is found in tones of red, green, yellow, and brown. Specimens with a combination of multicolored jasper and agate are especially pleasing to the eye. Clear to yellow calcite can be found in combination with agate or found inside amygdules found in basalt. Smash open any suspect basalt with a heavy hammer or geology pick to expose fresh cavities. The pyrite is found in the same manner, but is less common.

As with most river and creek collecting, you will have more gravel to hunt on during low water levels. Bring good mucking shoes and a change of clothes. The good gravel always seems to be on the other side of the creek. Make sure to do some exploring to find more access points to the creek. Many of the campgrounds found in the area have good creek access, so be sure to check them out.

Inspecting the gravels at Jones Creek for agates.

7. Wilson River

A sample of agate, jasper, porphyry basalt, and zeolite found at the Wilson River.

See map on page 16.
Land type: Riverbed gravels
County: Tillamook
GPS: N45 35.245' / W123 33.104', 544 ft.
Best season: Late spring–fall
Land manager: ODF—Tillamook State Forest
Material: Zeolites, jasper, agate
Tools: Geology pick, hammer
Vehicle: Any
Accommodations: Camping throughout Tillamook State Forest
Special attraction: Tillamook Forest Center
Finding the site: This site can be reached via OR 6, coming from either Tillamook or Portland. Turn onto Jones Creek Road, between mileposts 22 and 23 on OR 6, and take an immediate right into the Smith Homestead Day Use Area. At the back of the parking lot is the trailhead to Meadow Trail. Follow this trail approximately 0.1 to 0.2 mile until the woods open up and you begin to see some overgrown paths leading down to some gravel deposits. You can also follow the trail to the end where it will lead to yet even more gravel deposits in and adjacent to the Wilson River.

Hunting for agates on the Wilson River.

Rockhounding

Cutting through the coast range and the Tillamook State Forest is the beautiful and scenic Wilson River. This waterway is very popular with anglers and has many great swimming holes. To top it all off, there are good rocks in the abundant gravel deposits all along the river. The site mentioned here is the easiest to access. You can also find your own pullout or side road. Anything along the river with accessible gravel is worth checking out. I quite often stop at this site on my way to and from the ocean. It's not far off the highway and any vehicle can make it to the parking lot.

Search the massive gravel deposits for zeolites, jasper, agate, petrified wood, and pyrite. The zeolites are generally found as small amygdules in basalt. Use a good hammer to crack the basalt open, hopefully exposing fresh tiny crystals. The jasper tends to be brick-red, but some yellow and green may be found as well. The agate is generally clear, gray, or light blue. Some of it will have good banding. The petrified wood is generally low grade, but with some luck some good, hard pieces can be obtained. Some of the basalt you crack open may even have some pyrite in it. My friend and fellow rockhound, Kelly Langford, located a nice pyrite exposure in the river bedrock near the parking lot.

Lots of people use this river, and even though they may not be rockhounding, no one can really help but pick up a pretty shiny agate glistening in the water. Try to get away from the populated areas on the river. We found a lot more agate when we hiked far away from the popular spots. Be sure to bring some good river shoes for searching gravel that is still underwater and to better access gravel bars on the other side of the river.

8. Lolo Pass

A fractured, yet large piece of jasper-replaced petrified wood found in the hills of Lolo Pass. I fell down the hill immediately after taking this picture.

Land type: Mountain hills
County: Clackamas
GPS: N45 24.962' / W121 50.071', 2,815 ft.
Best season: Avoid winter snow
Land manager: USFS—Mt. Hood National Forest
Material: Petrified wood
Tools: Geology pick, hammer, chisel
Vehicle: Any
Accommodations: Campgrounds, RV parks, and motels throughout area; Timberline Lodge
Special attraction: Timberline Lodge
Finding the site: The site is easily reached from US 26 coming from either Portland or Madras. Head to Zig Zag and take East Lolo Pass Road. Drive 8.3 miles to a pullout on your right. The road cut is across the road from here. The waterfalls are back down the road at the bend, just before the pullout.

Mt. Hood

Look for a pullout near this waterfall, where you can begin your explorations of Lolo Pass. Be prepared to do some forest exploring for outcrops.

Rockhounding

Petrified wood can be found in the pyroclastic flows located in the Lolo Pass area near Zig Zag. Most is highly carbonized or of low quality, but occasionally pieces replaced by hard jasper can be found. The jasper can be in the cream, green, and yellow tones and makes great specimen pieces. The harder stuff is great for lapidary projects.

There are areas of exposed pyroclastic flows throughout the hills here, but not much is accessible to the general public. The site listed here is a good place to gain legal access and to get familiar with the material. The flow is exposed in the road cut and wood can be found in it. I wouldn't recommend digging in the road cut, as the forest service generally frowns on this and will sometimes hand out tickets for it. Stick to float collecting here.

There is another great exposure up a steep and tricky trail starting at the waterfall near the road. I wouldn't recommend it for children. Follow this trail up the creek to another waterfall flowing over a pyroclastic flow exposure. The size of the cliff and the amount of loose rock is intimidating. A hardhat would be a good idea if planning on spending any time near the wall. I found a couple of nice green jasper-replaced pieces of wood around here.

If you're in good physical shape, explore some of the faint trails leading into the woods from here. You can also try your luck hiking down the many trails found in the area. Look for good exposed rocky areas where there is not a lot of flora or tree debris. If you do happen to stumble upon a motherlode, remember your petrified wood collecting rules and leave some for other rockhounds.

9. Clackamette Park

A small agate found nestled in the river gravels at Clackamette Park in Oregon City.

See map on page 35.

Land type: Riverbank gravels

County: Clackamas

GPS: N45 22.337' / W122 36.161', 39 ft.

Best season: Any

Land manager: City of Oregon City (park); BLM—Salem (river)

Material: Quartz, agate, jasper, petrified wood

Tool: Geology pick

Vehicle: Any

Accommodations: RV park on site; lodging in Oregon City and Portland

Special attraction: Oregon Trail Museum

Finding the site: Clackamette Park is located just about where US 205 meets OR 99 in Oregon City. From this point take S.E. McLoughlin Boulevard to Dunes Drive. You'll know it when you see the golden arches. Drive about 300 feet and take a right onto Clackamette Drive. Travel 0.1 mile where you will take a left into the park. Drive all the way to the back by the boat launch and park. The boat launch leads into the Clackamas River.

Rockhounding

Clackamette Park is located where the Clackamas River dumps into the Willamette River. The Clackamas River is well known for its agate, jasper, and petrified wood. Anything that has survived the long, bumpy trip on this river is very hard and will take an excellent polish. The stones found here are well rounded and very smooth. My GPS mark was taken by the boat launch that enters the Clackamas. There are good gravel accumulations along this stretch. Be sure to check the Willamette side of the park too, as there are usually good deposits here also.

Lots of very interesting white to yellow quartz can be found. It looks best wet or polished. It would look nice in a small water feature like a fountain. The agate tends to be clear, but some blue tones occur with banding. Carnelian is rare, but not impossible. The jasper tends to be red, green, brown, or a combination of two or more colors. The wood that has made it this far is so rounded, it can be tricky to identify. Look for growth rings. There is also lots of interesting brecciated material that is very aesthetically appealing.

Across the river is Meldrum Bar Park, which provides a bit more access to gravel accumulations. The gravel bars on this side are mostly on the Willamette side and are very popular spots for anglers. Much of the gravel is occupied by those trying to get a bite; be sure to keep clear of their cast. The Willamette is a good place to hunt if gravels are exposed. From Clackamette Park all the way to Portland can be productive. The Willamette River near Oaks Bottom Park has been the source of many nice carnelians over the years.

A view of OR 99 crossing the Clackamas River at Clackamette Park. Search the gravels for agate, jasper, and petrified wood.

10. Clackamas River

A 3-inch agate found trying to hide underneath a larger rock at Site A of the Clackamas River. Be sure to inspect all sides of large rocks.

See map on page 35.

Land type: Forested riverbank

County: Clackamas

GPS: A: N45 11.985' / W 122 13.535', 686 ft. (large pullout); B: N45 11.516' / W122 12.694', 752 ft. (Memaloose Bridge parking area)

Best season: Summer

Land manager: USFS—Mt. Hood National Forest

Material: Agate, jasper, calcite, zeolites, siderite, common opal, petrified wood

Tools: Geology pick, hammer

Vehicle: Any

Accommodations: Camping throughout Mt. Hood National Forest along Clackamas River

Special attractions: Bagby Hot Springs; Austin Hot Springs

Finding the site: From Main Street in Estacada, head 8.5 miles east on OR 224 E/ Clackamas Highway. Site A is a large pullout on the right (south) side of the road. You'll see many short trails from the parking area. Site B is reached by continuing east on OR 224 for 0.9 mile to the Memaloose Bridge on National Forest Road (NF) 45. Cross the bridge over the river and park. The river is easily accessible from the parking area.

A view of the gravel bar found at Site A of the Clackamas River.

Rockhounding

The Clackamas River is a general location more than a specific site. The areas marked are just a couple of the many good places to get started. Pretty much anywhere you can safely park and find accessible gravel bars is the place to be. Summer is the best season for collecting as the water level is low and much more mineral-bearing gravel is exposed. Collecting is possible during the rest of the year, but you'll have much less exposed gravel to pick from. I've been out there in January and have done okay. For great examples of what you can find in the Clackamas River and nearby tributaries, make a stop at the Mossy Rock shop on Broadway in Estacada.

Most material here can be picked up as you find it. The agate is generally clear to yellow, some with banding. The jasper ranges in color from brown to green to red. The agate and jasper can be very river worn. Look for little indentations in these minerals that look as if someone were poking their fingernail into it. This is a sign of good silica content, a major component of agate and jasper. Petrified wood here generally has good grain replacement and is usually brown, gray, and or black. Some will take a good polish. Wood that doesn't take much of a polish can be interesting as specimen pieces.

For golden calcite rhombs, siderite, common opal, and zeolite material, you're going to have to break open a lot of rock. Look for gray to black basalt with evidence of amygdules on the surface. These little pockets in the rock are a sign that something untouched by weather could be hiding inside. Break open suspect rocks with your geology pick or three- to four-pound hammer. Sometimes multiple minerals can be revealed in the same host rock.

Avoid wading in the Clackamas River for specimens. The current can be dangerous, especially for small children. Stick to the abundant gravel bars you can easily reach. Camping at designated campsites along the river can offer more opportunities for gravel bar access.

11. Fish Creek

Look for basalt containing filled vugs and start cracking them open with a heavy hammer. Specimens here are small, but can be amazing under a hand lens.

See map on page 35.

Land type: Pine forest road cut; creek bed

County: Clackamas

GPS: N45 09.656' / W122 08.966', 1,055 ft.

Best season: Late spring–fall

Land manager: USFS—Mt. Hood National Forest

Material: Zeolites, calcite, chalcedony, agate, siderite, jasper, quartz, petrified wood

Tools: Hammer, chisel, gad

Vehicle: Any

Accommodations: Camping throughout Mt. Hood National Forest along the Clackamas River

Special attractions: Bagby Hot Springs; Austin Hot Springs

Finding the site: From Main Street in Estacada, follow OR 224 E/Clackamas Highway 14.9 miles into the Mt. Hood National Forest. Take a right (south) onto NF 54 (Fish Creek Road). Immediately find a safe place to pull off the road and park. If you want to park at the Fish Creek boat launch, there is a day use fee. The digging site is in the talus just northeast of the OR 224 and NF 54 (Fish Creek Road) junction.

Searching the basalt for mineral-filled vugs at the road cut found near Fish Creek.

Rockhounding

Minerals here are generally small, but very interesting. The calcite crystals form in a wide variety of habits. The chalcedony can form in stalactites. Most of the quartz crystals are small, but sparkle beautifully. It's a great location for micromount collectors. The best collecting is done in the talus on the north side of the highway, where I made my GPS marking. Because you will be adjacent to the road at this location, I would suggest not bringing children or dogs. There is also material on the south side of the road, in the middle of a hill that is very steep and not a great place for children to tag along. Take care not to knock rocks into the road.

Finding material here involves breaking open chunks of basalt to reveal small amygdules, hopefully filled in by an array of beautiful minerals. A three- to five-pound hammer works best, but if you're comfortable with a geology pick, that will work too. Wear eye protection while hammering away at rocks or near someone who is. I had my chin split open here from rock shrapnel. I'm just glad it wasn't my eye. Some material like the agate and quartz can be ever-so-carefully hammered out of the matrix, while more fragile specimens like zeolites and calcite look nice when still in matrix. In either case, take care when cleaving the basalt. You can easily destroy a great specimen with one wrong swing of the hammer.

Along Fish Creek you can find agates, jasper, and petrified wood. Access is easily gained from the boat launch near the day use parking lot. In his book *A Family Field Collecting Guide for Northwest Oregon and Southwest Washington*, Jon Gladwell reports a fossil leaf imprint locality about 4 miles south and across Fish Creek. The road leading back there was washed out in the 1996 floods. I've hiked in about 2 miles back, but I always seem to get distracted while exploring the many creeks along the path. If you're up for a long hike and some exploring, give it a try.

12. Collawash River

Sun-bleached petrified wood and a multicolored piece of jasp-agate found at Site A of the Collawash River. Petrified wood approximately 4 inches long.

See map on page 35.

Land type: Forested riverbank

County: Clackamas

GPS: A: N45 01.961' / W122 03.635', 1,460 ft. (Riverford Campground); B: N44 59.470' / W122 03.712', 1,606 ft. (Big Fan Campground)

Best season: Any; avoid winter snow

Land manager: USFS—Mt. Hood National Forest

Material: Agate, jasper, petrified wood

Tool: Geology pick

Vehicle: Any

Accommodations: Camping throughout Mt. Hood National Forest

Special attractions: Bagby Hot Springs; Austin Hot Springs

Finding the site: From Main Street in Estacada, travel east on OR 224 (Clackamas Highway) for about 25.3 miles where you will take a slight right onto NF 46. Travel 3.7 miles to where you will take a right onto NF 63 (Collawash River Road). At this junction you will immediately see a very small pullout on your immediate right.

This is Site A where the Collawash enters the Clackamas. Park here and hike your way a bit down the road where you will find a trail leading through Riverford Campground. Walk through the campground until you reach the river gravels. Site B is reached by continuing along NF 63 for another 3.3 miles where you will find a pullout on your left. There will be some boulders blocking a road that leads into Big Fan Campground. Walk about 0.2 mile through the campground to the gravel deposits.

Rockhounding

The Collawash River is a tributary to the Clackamas and also provides much of its petrified wood. I want to thank my friends and fellow rockhounds Nate and Tammie Macalevy who turned me on to this great collecting site. We all met on the Facebook group Northwest Diehard Rockhounds, which is proof positive that joining a rock club/group is a good thing.

The GPS sites listed are just a couple places we found to pull out near good gravel bars. Do some diligent searching and maybe you'll find your own special spot. Site A is a small pullout near a bridge and a campground where the Collawash enters the Clackamas. Technically you'll be collecting on the Clackamas at this site, but the wood pushed out on the gravel bars is most likely from the Collawash. Park and cut through the campground to find one

Search the abundant gravels of the Collawash River for petrified wood, jasper, and agate. This is Site A, where the Collawash meets the Clackamas.

of many trails leading to the gravel bars. Site B is found by hiking maybe a quarter mile through an old campground to find the river. The gravels at Site B are extensive and should provide plenty of area for the curious rockhound to roam.

The wood is generally porous, but some pieces can be dense enough to cut and polish. Even the porous pieces have good grain replacement and color. The color of the wood tends to be very wood colored (browns and grays) to black tones. I have seen people use bleach to lighten and brighten cut slabs of darker material.

The agate is generally small and found in mostly clear to yellow tones. Some can have banding. The jasper can be red, green, brown, or a combination of colors. With diligent searching and some luck, somewhat large pieces can be obtained. Some of the jasper can be brecciated or have veins of agate running through it.

The Collawash River is located very close to the very popular Bagby Hot Springs, a wonderful place to have a nice soak. Make sure to save some time during your visit to make a stop. They have updated the tubs recently and are taking great care to make sure the hot springs are a safe and comfortable place to soak for many years to come. It is definitely worth the fee and short hike in.

13. North Santiam River

Agate and jasper found along the banks of the North Fork Santiam River.

Land type: Riverbed gravels
County: Marion
GPS: N44 47.505' / W122 47.703', 435 ft.
Best season: Summer–fall
Land manager: BLM—Salem
Material: Jasper, petrified wood, agate
Tool: Geology pick
Vehicle: Any
Accommodations: None on site; lodging and RV parks in Stayton
Special attractions: Silver Falls; Detroit Lake
Finding the site: From I-5 in Salem, take OR 22 east and exit at Stayton. Be sure to take the main exit and not the truck route exit. Travel south through Stayton on 1st Avenue (Cascade Highway) for about 1.6 miles until you are about to reach a bridge. There will be a short road on your left leading down to a parking area. Park here and hike your way along under the bridge until you reach the river and her gravel deposits. On the southeast end of the bridge is a boat launch, but no gravel.

Willamette Valley

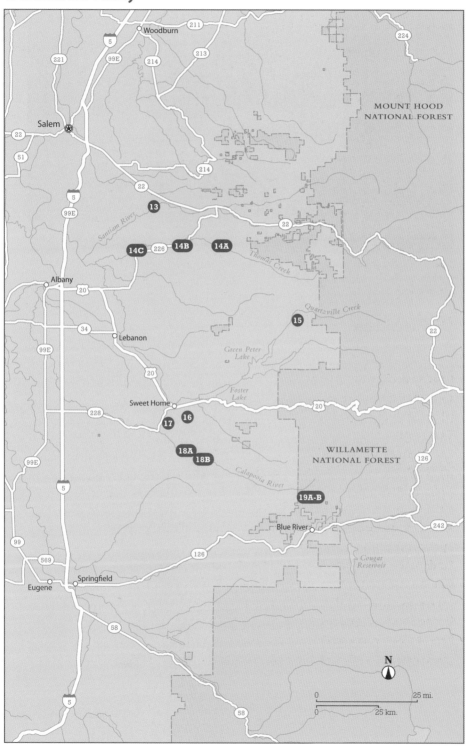

Search for agate, jasper, and petrified wood in the abundant gravel deposits of the North Fork Santiam River.

Rockhounding

A very large gravel deposit is located at this point in the Santiam River found on the edge of Stayton. There is a short walk from the parking area to the river gravels. The hike in will also bring you across gravels pushed around by flood-waters. Don't neglect exploring these deposits on your hike in or out. The material at this site is not particularly abundant, but being such a short distance from Salem and I-5, this easily accessible rockhounding location makes for a nice day trip. It's also a great place to bring the whole family for a picnic. Pack a lunch and bring some water because you can definitely spend a lot of time exploring this expansive gravel bar.

Search the gravel deposits for the usual Oregon suspects: agate, jasper, and petrified wood. The material is mostly tumbler size, but the occasional large piece can be happened upon with a bit of luck. The agate found here is generally clear to a blue-gray tone, some with banding. The jasper is mostly dark to bright red, but green and brown tones can be found as well. The petrified wood is mostly small, but is generally hard and will take a great polish when tumbled. A good rain really helps to differentiate quality lapidary material from porous junk. Luckily there's a river right there to wash off any suspect material during dry and dusty days.

14. Thomas Creek

This nice big agate was just waiting for me to pick it up at Thomas Creek.

See map on page 47.

Land type: Gravel creek bed

County: Linn

GPS: A: N44 42.728' / W122 36.620', 811 ft. (gravels near bridge); B: N44 42.730' / W122 43.184', 480 ft. (Hannah Bridge); C: N44 42.265' / W122 50.814', 300 ft. (Scio Historical Depot Museum park)

Best season: Summer–fall

Land manager: BLM—Salem

Material: Agate, jasper, petrified wood, calcite

Tool: Geology pick

Vehicle: Any

Accommodations: Lodging in Albany; camping and RV parks near Scio

Special attractions: Silver Falls; Detroit Lake

Finding the site: From I-5 in Salem, take OR 22 east to Mehama. Take the OR 226 exit and follow it about 1.3 miles through Lyons where it will take a sharp turn heading west out of town. Continue along OR 226 for another 5.5 miles where you will take a left (east) onto Thomas Creek Drive. Follow this road for 4.4 miles where

A view of the bridge from Site A at Thomas Creek. Search the gravel for good agate, jasper, and petrified wood.

you will encounter a bridge with a gate. Park near the bridge, but make sure not to block it. Site A is reached by navigating your choice of two steep access trails and hiking your way downstream to the gravel deposits. Site B is reached by heading back to OR 226 and continuing another 2.6 miles to Camp Morrison Drive. Take a left, cross the historic covered bridge, and park in the pulloff to your immediate right. The trail to the river is right by the bridge. Avoid the private land. Hike downstream over the bedrock and cross a small creek to access the gravel deposits. Site C is reached by continuing along OR 226 6.5 miles into Scio, where you will take a right onto Main Street and then another right onto N.E. 1st Avenue. Drive to and park at the park next to the Scio Historical Museum. The gravels are easily accessed from here.

Rockhounding

Thomas Creek is a great place to make a day trip and do some rockhounding. The creek is easily accessible from I-5 and can be reached quickly from Portland or Eugene. The sites listed can be driven to in any vehicle. The only drawback to this creek is the trails accessing the creek from the parking areas. They can be a bit steep and precarious to get down. Some bushwhacking may be called for at Site A. If you're in good physical condition and are up for the challenge of climbing over and through things, then this is a great spot for you.

The creek is littered with agate, jasper, and petrified wood. The agate is plentiful and sizeable. It is mostly clear, but gray to blue shades are common and some light carnelian can be found as well. The jasper is mostly red but generally bright. It can also be found in tones of yellow, brown, green, and multicolored. Most of it is very hard and will take an excellent polish. Oligocene petrified wood is fairly common in this creek and is found in mostly brown and black tones. The calcite tends to be in pockets of other rocks such as agate or basalt.

Site A has a large gravel deposit forming a sort of island in the creek. A decent portion of the gravels are easily accessible, but much of it is only reachable by crossing the creek many times and a fair amount of bushwhacking. In my humble opinion it's all worth it. Low water levels are best for better gravel exposure, but I have found great material here even in early February. Sites B and C are pretty much inaccessible during high waters. Fording the creek at Site B is virtually impossible during the winter and spring months. The gravels at Site C are pretty much covered during these months as well, so be sure to plan your visit accordingly. Don't forget your mucking shoes and a good collecting bag. As usual, a bit of rain helps wash off the dust and makes the good silicate material shine, so don't let a poor weather forecast deter you.

15. Boulder Creek

Boulder Creek pyrite crystals perched in matrix. Largest crystal approximately ¼ inch.

See map on page 47.

Land type: Forested road cut

County: Linn

GPS: N44 34.171' / W122 23.084', 1,877 ft.

Best season: Late spring–fall

Land manager: USFS—Mount Hood National Forest

Material: Pyrite

Tool: Geology pick

Vehicle: Any

Accommodations: Primitive camping along Quartzville Creek; lodging in Sweet Home

Special attraction: Over the Rivers and Through the Woods Scenic Byway

Finding the site: From Sweet Home travel east on US 20 for approximately 5.5 miles. Take a left (north) onto Quartzville Road. From here continue on the road for 20.3 miles, where you will see a bridge to your left (south). Cross the bridge and take the fork to the left. Continue 1.6 miles uphill until you encounter a large white rust-stained road cut on your left.

Rockhounding:

The good news: This site is accessible by any vehicle and material is easily obtained. The bad news: You're going to get muddy, and I've heard reports of the mud containing very small traces of cyanide. Wear clothes and shoes you don't mind getting dirty and have some to change into after collecting. Bring an old towel to wipe off any mud you don't want getting all over your vehicle's interior. The interior of my truck has been permanently stained with this mud for many years. I see it as a sort of battle scar. Others see it as just a mess. The choice is yours. The most important choice to make is to wash your hands after collecting and definitely before eating.

The mud in the road cut found near Boulder Creek is full of small brassy pyrite (fools' gold) crystals formed in the classic pyriteohedron or dodeca-hedron crystal habit. The crystals range in size from ⅛ inch to about ½ inch. Pieces of matrix containing multiple crystals can make especially beautiful specimen pieces. The best material is of course found in the wettest, muddiest spots in the road cut. Spend some time hunting the biggest, most completely formed crystals that have worked their way out of the hill. Take caution with the precarious boulders lurking high above the road cut. I wouldn't want to be in the area when they finally tumbled down.

Nearby Quartzville Creek is a recreational gold panning area set aside by the BLM and is very popular with gold hunters. I caught gold fever for the first time while panning on this creek. Flour gold can be found in and around the creek in the black sands. Feeding Quartzville Creek are both Thistle Creek and Whitcomb Creek, both known for their fine agates, but they have limited, if any access. If you have time, check on accessibility to these sites when in the area. Some years there have been "no trespassing" signs and closed gates; other years, no signs and open gates.

Picking out some excellent dodecahedron pyrite crystals at Boulder Creek. I had good luck to the right of the photo.

16. Ames Creek

A sample of petrified wood found in Ames Creek. Watch for wood grain while walking the creek.

See map on page 47.

Land type: Forested creek bed

County: Linn

GPS: N44 22.641' / W122 41.848', 684 ft.

Best season: Summer

Land manager: BLM—Salem; BLM—Eugene

Material: Petrified wood

Tools: Geology pick (for prying), collecting bag

Vehicle: Any

Accommodations: Camping near Green Peter Dam and Quartzville Creek; lodging in Sweet Home

Special attraction: Over the Rivers and Through the Woods Scenic Byway

Finding the site: From US 20 through Sweet Home, take 18th Avenue south about a half mile until it turns into Ames Creek Road. Continue on Ames Creek Road for 1.5 miles to a pulloff on the right (west) side of the road. Park here and locate the trail that leads down to the creek.

Rockhounding

Ames Creek is a fairly easily accessible location to collect Oligocene petrified wood. Any vehicle can make it to the pulloff, where you can begin your search. The only drawback is you have to scramble your way down a small, yet heavily vegetated hillside to the creek. The GPS reading I took was at the beginning of one of the easier trails leading to the creek. There are other deer trails along the road that you can follow, but they are much steeper and overgrown. Wear old shoes you don't mind getting wet or rubber boots for mucking around in the creek.

Search up and down the creek for the telltale signs of petrified wood such as growth rings and bark patterns. Most of the wood found is fairly porous, but the occasional harder piece can be obtained and will take a nice polish. The wood tends to be in brown or gray tones, some being completely black. I find when hunting petrified wood in wooded creeks and rivers I get constantly fooled by pieces of real wood stuck in between the rocks. If you find this happening to you as well, don't give up. Being diligent and inspecting all suspect pieces should reward rockhounds with a fair amount of material. On one visit I found a very small but very red piece of carnelian. Chandler Mountain is nearby and is well known for its excellent carnelian. Unfortunately accessing Chandler Mountain is difficult to impossible these days. I'm sure a few pieces have slipped into the stream, but don't hold your breath.

When the river starts slowing down late in the summer season, a brown slime starts coating the rocks in the river making it much more difficult to identify wood, or anything else. Plus once you start stirring it up, it clouds the water making it next to impossible to see anything. Plan your trip accordingly to make the best of your river time.

Look for this pullout and locate a decent trail that leads down to Ames Creek. Bring your mucking shoes!

17. Holleywood Ranch

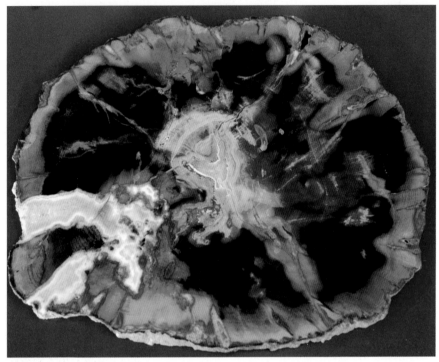

A cut and polished section of petrified wood found on the Holleywood Ranch.
Photo by David Bauer. Holleywood Ranch collection.

See map on page 47.

Land type: Pits in ranch field

County: Linn

GPS: N44 21.811' / W122 45.301', 734 ft.

Best season: Spring – summer.

Land manager: Private—Holleywood Ranch

Material: Petrified wood, agate limb casts

Tools: Pick, shovel, pry bar

Vehicle: Any

Accommodations: Primitive camping allowed on site; camping available near Green Peter Reservoir and Quartzville Creek; RV parks in Sweet Home

Special attraction: Over the Rivers and Through the Woods Scenic Byway

Finding the site: From I-5 take exit 216 and head east on OR 228 (Halsey–Sweet Home Highway). Travel about 15 miles until you reach the town of Holley. Turn right onto Old Holley Road and follow it for 1.8 miles. The Holleywood Ranch will be on your left. Drive past the house and park near the portable toilet. The site is also accessible from Sweet Home taking OR 228 (Halsey–Sweet Home Highway).

Rockhounding

The Holleywood Ranch is located in a hotbed of petrified wood deposits found in the area between Holley and Sweet Home. This fee-based dig offers Oregon rockhounds a rare chance to access high-quality material otherwise heavily guarded by private land. Not only is there great wood to be found, but the owners of the Holleywood Ranch are very warm and inviting. Brad Newport is usually on site and is ready and willing to answer any questions you may have.

Once at the ranch you can choose to dig or pick previously dug pieces from the "bone pile." Brad does a great job exposing fresh ground for visitors, making digging much easier. Bring a shovel, pry bar, and a probe to assist in your efforts. The ranch sometimes has tools for loan, but they get nabbed up pretty quickly if others are visiting unprepared. Finding the wood is the easy part. Deciding which high-quality pieces to bring home is the tough part. The wood is of such high quality that the ranch was featured on the Travel Channel's show *Cash & Treasures.*

So far sixty-five different species of wood from the ranch have been identified. There are too many to list here. The 2.6- to 65-million-year-old petrified woods found here are hard, have great cellular replacement, and take a great polish. Pieces weighing up to several hundred pounds

Rarely beautiful carnelian limb casts can be found at the Holleywood Ranch.
Photo by David Bauer. Holleywood Ranch collection

can be obtained with a bit of luck and a lot of hard work. Agate limb casts can be found and some are even replaced by carnelian. Pieces containing quartz and even rarely amethyst can be obtained. The variety seems limitless.

The ranch was once known as the Marker Ranch and many paleobotanical studies have been conducted over the years on the wood found in the area. For more information about the many varieties of petrified wood found on the ranch, check out *The Ore Bin,* April 1968, Vol. 30, No. 4. They have a list of fifty-four of the sixty-five species found and list some theories about how so many varieties of wood ended up in one place.

The Holleywood Ranch is open year-round (weather permitting). Many local rock clubs visit the ranch on weekends. If you want a more private digging experience, try to plan your visit for weekdays. Expect to pay a per pound fee with a total dollar minimum for ages 12 and up. Discounts are available for groups of ten or more. Primitive camping is allowed on site. The Newports also own a couple of restaurants in Sweet Home that are very welcoming to rockhounds. More information about the Holleywood Ranch can be found at www.holleywoodranch.com or by writing 26250 Old Holley Road, Sweet Home, OR, 97386; (541) 401-0899.

The Holleywood Ranch regularly exposes fresh ground for digging petrified wood. Bring shovels and probes if you have them.

18. Calapooia River

Search the Calapooia River for agate, jasper, petrified wood, and rare Holley Blue Agate.

See map on page 47.

Land type: Forested riverbank

County: Linn

GPS: A: N44 18.667' / W122 42.578', 718 ft. (bridge); B: N44 17.741' / W122 39.189', 813 ft. (pullout)

Best season: Summer

Land manager: BLM—Eugene

Material: Petrified wood, agate, jasper

Tools: Geology pick, collecting bag

Vehicle: Any

Accommodations: Primitive camping near Green Peter Dam and Quartzville Creek; lodging in Sweet Home

Special attraction: Over the Rivers and Through the Woods Scenic Byway

Finding the site: From US 20 in Sweet Home take OR 228 south to Holley about 4.8 miles, where you will take a left onto Calapooia River Road. Travel 5.4 miles to Site A found on your right. Park at the bridge and find the trail leading to the river. Site B is located by continuing another 3.4 miles down Calapooia River Road to a pullout on your right.

Rockhounding

This area was once a rockhound's dream collecting area. The Calapooia River is home to one of the famous Holley Blue Agate deposits. It has been off limits for years, but you could always hope for lighter sun-bleached pieces found in river gravels. Many great petrified wood deposits are found scattered along the river, adding to the mix. There's even a thunderegg deposit back there, which is rare in western Oregon.

This is the only piece of Holley Blue I have ever found in the Calapooia River. Don't hold your breath; it is very rare.

It saddens me to report that this very productive river is now mostly off limits to collecting, or much of anything else for that matter. The Weyerhaeuser lumber firm now has most of the access roads on lockdown. When I first visited this river in 2006, I saw my first "no rockhounding" signs. Upon my visit here in the early spring of 2012, I was deterred by a very large sign, suggesting that I should not stop anywhere on the road. There was a gate, it was open, but I didn't want to risk getting locked in. The river was too high at the time anyway. I returned in late summer and the gate was closed and locked. There is however still some public access to the river and due to its great material it is still worth listing.

The GPS sites are just two places I found that provide legal river access. There were more small pulloffs, but they were occupied by vehicles during my GPS reconnaissance. Use my directions or find your own spot to safely park. There was evidence of gold mining claims along the river, so be on the lookout for markers. Both lumber companies and gold miners do not take trespassing lightly. Under no circumstances should you trespass on their land.

Collecting here is the same as any other river. Be on the lookout for well worn material. The agate is mostly clear and banding is common. Be on the lookout for anything that may be the famed Holley Blue. If you're very lucky it won't be too sun bleached. The petrified wood is very bright and can be found in many tones. Look for growth rings and angled material. Very bright red, sometimes brecciated jasper can be found in the river too.

Pay attention to the access availability over the coming years. With any luck, rockhounds will be able to get back into this once very productive river.

19. Gold Hill

A sizeable light amethyst quartz point found near the Poorman Mine. Only the tip of the crystal was showing above the surface of the road. There are lots of icebergs at Gold Hill.

See map on page 47.

Land type: Mountain ridge forest

County: Linn/Lane

GPS: A: N44 13.486' / W122 21.257', 4,054 ft. (Poorman Mine); B: N44 13.240' / W122 20.989', 4,420 ft. (Below Infinity Mine)

Best season: Summer

Land manager: USFS—Willamette National Forest

Material: Quartz crystals, some amethyst

Tools: Geology pick, hammer, gad, chisel, rake

Vehicle: 4WD suggested

Accommodations: Primitive camping near Blue Reservoir

Special attractions: Blue Reservoir; Cougar Hot Springs

Finding the site: If traveling via I-5, use exit 194 to Springfield and head east on OR 126 (McKenzie Highway) for about 43 miles. Drive past Blue River and turn north onto Old Scout Road, which becomes NF 15. Drive about 4.4 miles and take the road to the left onto NF 1509. After 0.3 mile turn left onto NF 1510. Drive about 7.8 miles and take a left onto NF 2820. After about 0.6 mile you will come to a fork. About 1.6 miles down the road to the right you will find the Poorman Mine (Site A). To the left is the Infinity Mine (Site B), found 1.1 miles down this road.

You will encounter many beautiful views like this on your drive up to Gold Hill. Be sure to bring a camera.

Rockhounding

Quartz crystals are the prize found at Gold Hill; some even come with a light amethyst hue. Material here tends to be small, around a half inch, but larger crystals can be obtained with diligent searching. Sally found a 2-inch double terminated crystal very close to the Poorman Mine. It was an "iceberg," showing only a small amount of the tip above the soil. Be sure to inspect even the smallest pieces. My GPS markings were taken close to mines that were productive in the past or are currently under claim. Access to these sites can be very limited. I've been back here in late May and was forced to turn around due to snow on the road. Plan to visit during hot summer months.

The barred adit that was once the Poorman Mine (Site A) is easily spotted from the road leading in. Park at the turnaround up the hill and begin your search here. Chips of quartz can be found littered all over the road leading in. Timing your search with the sun shining on the road will help with your hunt. Hunting the hillsides in this area can be productive, but finding spots not completely covered in pine needles can prove to be difficult. A rake may be a helpful tool in this area.

B is located just below the active Infinity Mine. There was evidence of people digging in the hillside. They must have been onto something, because there was a lot of dirt moved. I poked around the holes and found a few chips of quartz, but the sun was out in full force and I wasn't up to doing any digging. Long ago I purchased some very nice large skeletal quartz crystals that came out of the Infinity Mine when it was open in the past. Perhaps it will be available to the public again in the future.

20. Moolack Beach

Moolack Beach is a great place to find marine fossils, agates, and jaspers.

Land type: Coastal beach gravels
County: Lincoln
GPS: A: N44 42.250' / W124 03.671', 55 ft. (large parking area); B: N44 42.121' / W124 03.685', 48 ft. (small pullout)
Best season: Winter–late spring
Land manager: BLM
Material: Agate, jasper, petrified wood, shell fossils, mammal bone fossils
Tools: Geology pick, gem scoop
Vehicle: Any
Accommodations: Camping and yurts at Beverly State Park; lodging in Lincoln City and Newport
Special attractions: Yaquina Head Lighthouse; Pacific Coast Scenic Byway
Finding the site: Moolack Beach is easily reached from two locations just off US 101, between mileposts 136 and 137. Site A is a large pulloff with plenty of parking and is well marked. There is a steep muddy trail leading to the beach on the north side of the parking lot. The second access point (Site B) is a smaller pulloff 0.2 mile south of the first. While this second location has less parking, the trail is much more accessible for the young, elderly, injured, or those who just don't want to get muddy on the trail located at the other pulloff. I list them

Central Coast

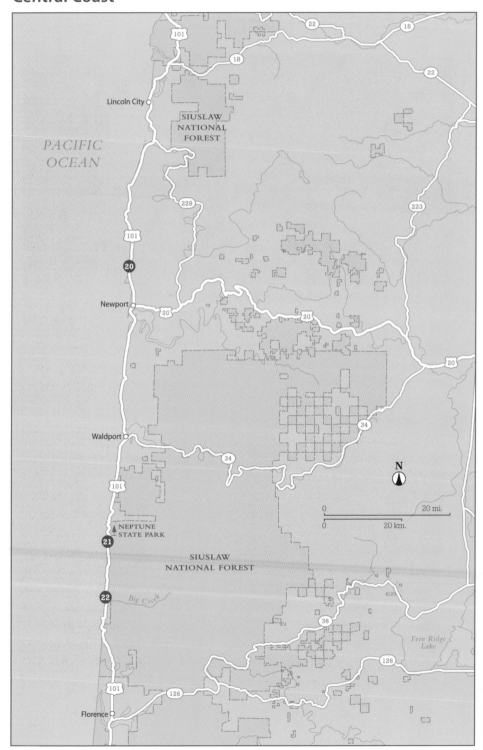

A perfect example of what not to do when collecting at the ocean. Never turn your back on her! Here I am getting hit by a sneaker wave at Moolack. Photo by Sally Franklin

separately because they are split by Moolack Creek, which can be difficult and unsafe to cross when on the beach. After arriving at the beach, determine where the best gravels are and then choose which site to enter from. If you have rubber boots, the tide is out, and the creek isn't very deep, then it shouldn't matter where you enter.

Rockhounding

Collecting here, like most Oregon coast beach locations, is just a matter of walking around and picking up rocks. Keep an eye on that Pacific Ocean, and never turn your back on her. She will get you wet. She will also sometimes try to steal your bucket full of tools and rocks if you leave it unattended near the surf. Trust me, I know from experience. Get to the beach after high tide and start collecting as the surf heads out. It's easier to find material when the gravel is wet, so don't let a rainy day deter you. A gem scoop is handy for getting things off the ground without straining your back. I also like to use a geology pick for moving rock around to expose fresh material. Great finds can be hidden beneath boring gray rocks. As usual, there is no digging in the sea walls as the ocean erodes the coast just fine on its own. Material here is abundant as long as the gravels are exposed. In the summer there's not much more than just sand.

If you're an agate lover like me, you'll really enjoy collecting at this site. At this beach I have found clear, yellow, carnelian, brown, banded, and even rare agatized "clam bellies" and elusive black agates here. "Clam bellies" are fossil casts of clam shells that decomposed after being covered by lava or ash and left a mold behind that was later filled in by agate. Many of them have enhydros. In fact, many of the agates on the Oregon coast have potential for enhydros. Check your haul with a flashlight, backlighting specimens to see if there's water in there. Black agates are very difficult to spot. Look for wet black rocks with a coating of white swirls, almost like they have bird guano on them.

The jasper here is no slouch either, in shades of red, orange, yellow, green, brown, and multicolored. Petrified wood can also be found here. Keep an eye out for growth rings. Fossil shells, mostly clams and gastropods, are strewn about as well. These beaches are well known for their fossil sea mammal bones including seals and whales; but remember, you need to have a permit to collect vertebrate fossils.

There are many other places nearby to find potentially productive beaches. If one beach isn't producing, move on to the next. These stops include Beverly Beach, Taft Beach, and Roads End. Taft Beach in Newport is known for its interesting tumbled zeolites.

21. Cummings Creek/Neptune State Park

A small sample of silicate materials found at Neptune State Park.

See map on page 64.

Land type: Ocean beach / creek gravels

County: Lane

GPS: N44 15.911' / W124 06.485', 19 ft.

Best season: Winter–late spring

Land manager: BLM—Eugene

Material: Agate, jasper, petrified wood, marine fossils

Tool: Geology pick

Vehicle: Any

Accommodations: Camping at nearby state parks

Special attraction: Pacific Coast Scenic Byway

Finding the site: Neptune State Park is located off of US 101 about 3 miles south of Yachats. Look for the sign and pull into the parking area. The trail leading to the beach is on the north end of the parking lot. Follow it to the beach.

A view of the parking lot and the abundant gravels at Neptune State Park. Plan on doing some hiking at this site.

Rockhounding

I think this beach is a lot of fun to collect at. There are usually good gravel deposits all the way from the mouth of Cummings Creek to at least a half mile south of the parking lot. For those in good physical condition, the south end provides a fun scramble over and through some mysterious and inviting rock formations that harbor small tide pools with colorful anemones and gravel accumulations. I like to think that those rocks keep a fair amount of people out, meaning more rocks for those of us who can clamber over and around them.

As with most beaches, expect to see some agate, jasper, and petrified wood. The agate can be in just about any color and pattern usually found on Oregon beaches. A copy of *Agates of the Oregon Coast* will help you identify the wide variety of agates available. It's a book every Oregon agate hunter should have in their collection. The jasper is typically red or green, but other colors can be found as well. Petrified wood is usually in the gray to brown tones. Fossil shells are fairly common and other marine fossils can be found imbedded in rock or concretions.

There are many other places to find potentially productive beaches nearby. Some of these stops include Strawberry Hill Wayside and Lost Creek State Park. The trail at Strawberry Hill leading to the ocean is pretty precarious and keeps a lot of people off the gravels below. Use extreme caution if planning on using this trail and hunting the gravels below.

22. Big Creek/Roosevelt Beach

A large agate that was waiting for me at the end of the trail leading to Big Creek. Specimen approximately 4 inches.

See map on page 64.

Land type: Ocean beach

County: Lane

GPS: N44 10.571' / W124 06.922', 17 ft.

Best season: Winter–late spring

Land manager: BLM—Eugene

Material: Agate, jasper, petrified wood, marine fossils, zeolites

Tools: Geology pick, hammer

Vehicle: Any

Accommodations: Camping at nearby state parks; lodging in Florence and Coos Bay

Special attraction: Pacific Coast Scenic Byway

Finding the site: Big Creek is located on US 101 between Yachats and Coos Bay. If traveling from Coos Bay, Big Creek is the next stop north of Muriel O. Ponsler Wayside. There is a bridge crossing the creek. Park on the northeast side of the bridge in the pullout area. The trail leading to the beach is across the highway. Use caution when crossing the highway, especially with children or dogs. Scramble your way down the trail to find the gravel deposits.

A view of US 101 crossing Big Creek. Park on the northeast side of the bridge. The trail is on the northwest side.

Rockhounding

First off you should know that there are a lot of creeks around Oregon named Big Creek. There are at least three on the coast that I know of. I can't speak for the others, but this particular Big Creek is a great place to do some agate hunting. The creek pushes a lot of good material out onto Roosevelt Beach year-round. Good gravel bars are usually exposed at the mouth of the winding creek. This is rare, as most Oregon beaches are covered by sand during the summer. I'm not promising that there will always be gravel—that's up to the weather—but it's a generally promising place to search for agates most of the year.

I've had good luck finding large fist-size agates at this site over the years. They tend to be clear to yellow, but the size makes up for the lack of color. That doesn't mean you're not going to find colorful agates. I've found many of those too. There's potential for just about any variety here including carnelian and black and fancy agates. The jasper tends to be red or green, but other colors are not unheard of. The petrified wood is usually gray to brown. Marine fossils can be found imbedded in rock or hidden inside concretions. Keep your eyes peeled for zeolite-filled amygdules in basalt. Bring a good hammer if you are interested in exposing fresh zeolites.

There are many other places to find potentially productive beaches nearby. Big Creek just happens to have decent gravel most of the year. These stops include Muriel O. Ponsler Wayside, Bobs Creek, China Creek, and Stonefield Recreation Area. If one beach isn't producing good gravel, move on to the next. It's a good idea to have a friend along while driving. You can watch the road and your friend can watch for gravel.

23. John Day River

A small sample of the minerals we collected during our first visit to the John Day River.

Land type: River gravels; ash deposits
County: Wheeler and Wasco
GPS: A: N44 55.160' / W120 28.264', 1,299 ft.; B: N 44 57.011' / W120 29.193', 1,272 ft.; C: N44 57.075' / W120 29.467', 1,322 ft.
Best season: Late spring–fall
Land manager: BLM—Prineville
Material: Chalcedony, agate, jasper, quartz, amethyst, petrified wood, zeolites, calcite, selenite, common opal, fossils
Tool: Geology pick
Vehicle: Site A: any; Sites B and C: 4WD
Accommodations: Camping allowed on BLM land
Special attractions: John Day National Monument; Fossil, Oregon
Finding the site: From either Antelope or Fossil, use OR 218 and travel to the bridge in Clarno. Site A is the recreation area easily reached on the east side of the bridge. Sites B and C are reached by taking the dirt road on the west side of the bridge by the grange hall. Take this road about 3.4 miles to a pullout/camping area on your right. Site C is at the ash deposits another 0.1 mile up the road and is easily seen from Site B.

North Central

A view of the John Day River and its plentiful gravels at Site B. Site C can be seen in the background.

Rockhounding

Laura Joki, of Rock Your World in Lincoln City, Oregon, recommended the calcite spot to me. It was an extremely hot day when Sally and I first visited. We couldn't help but lust after the cool, refreshing waters of the John Day River running below us as we scrambled the parched hillside of Site A. The allure of the river was accentuated by the inviting gravel bars. I'm sure glad we decided to investigate. We found a nice swimming hole near a bend in the river, marked as Site B, and spent half the day frolicking in the water and collecting abundant material.

Sites A and B are two spots we found with easy and legal river access. Do some exploring to find more river access. There is a lot of private land in the area, so be mindful where you explore. A boat would be a great way to explore the river and there just happens to be a boat launch at Site A, just off the highway and accessible by any vehicle. Site B requires some good clearance and 4WD, especially if the road is wet.

Search the gravels both in and out of the water for good silicate material. There is a ton of mostly clear and some blue chalcedony; some pieces can be quite large. We found many varieties of agate including banded, fortification banding, and brown moss. Some agates have crystalline quartz pockets. I found one especially nice piece with some light amethyst. Multiple colors of jasper can be found. We found green, red, and some swirly multicolored pieces. Look for good hard petrified wood, though it's not as common as the other materials.

Site C is an exposed ash deposit that can be easily seen from Site B. Search the hillside for orange to yellow calcite, selenite, tiny little agates, yellow-green common opal, and marine fossils. I didn't spend a whole lot of time exploring this area, as the river was much more inviting. I did however find pieces of everything listed and the site has a lot of potential for exploration.

24. Fossil

A metasequoia fossil commonly found in Fossil, Oregon. Hold out for complete specimens.

See map on page 72.
Land type: Small shale hillside.
County: Wheeler
GPS: N45 00.155' / W120 12.801', 2,707 ft.
Best season: Spring–fall
Land manager: Private—Wheeler High School
Material: Leaf fossils
Tools: Geology pick, paint scraper, packing materials
Vehicle: Any
Accommodations: Lodging in Fossil
Special attractions: Oregon Paleo Lands Institute; Journey Through Time Scenic Byway
Finding the site: Fossil can be reached by various roads from Antelope, Condon, Kimberly, or Mitchell. When you reach town the high school is easily found perched above the town. Check in and pay at the small shed found at the athletics field.

Rockhounding

Wheeler High School was built on a very productive fossil bed. Today the school allows lucky rockhounds to collect on their land for a small fee. At the time of publication, you were allowed to keep three of your best specimens.

They also have group rates. Please be sure to contact the school before visiting to ensure that they will be available for visitors. All funds raised from fossil collecting go toward school activities. As the son of a teacher, I can tell you that all public schools need every extra dollar they can get.

The fossils here are from the Bridge Creek Flora of the Oligocene John Day Formation. Leaves and needles are the most common fossils found here. My favorites are the abundant metasequoia needles, Oregon's State Fossil. More than forty different species of plants have been identified at this site including ancestors of modern sycamore, maple, oak, rose, and alder. Very rarely some aquatic vertebrate fossils such as fish and even a salamander have been recovered.

Digging is fairly easy at this location. Even better there is usually someone on site to explain things and help identify specimens. To get started pick yourself a good piece of shale. Take a chisel or even better a good paint scraper and wedge it into the side of a piece of shale. Lightly tap the end with a hammer. The goal is to split the shale open like an ancient book revealing a fossil-filled page in history. Open a lot of material and be picky and patient for whole-leaf specimens or pieces showing multiple specimens.

For more information about collecting fossils at Wheeler High School, please visit www.paleolands.org/find/time/here/C52, or contact them at 333 West 4th Street, PO Box 104, Fossil, OR, 97830; (541) 763-4303.

Sign in and pay at the shack, behind the high school in Fossil. Hike the trail seen on the right of the picture to the bare hill on the left of the picture.

25. Priday Polka-Dot Agate

When you arrive at the Priday Polka-Dot Agate beds, you won't be able to miss this well-known landmark.

See map on page 72.

Land type: High desert
County: Jefferson
GPS: N44 45.506' / W120 49.868', 3,066 ft.
Best season: Summer only
Land manager: Private—West Coast Mining
Material: Polka-dot agate
Tools: Hammer, chisel, gad, pick
Vehicle: Any
Accommodations: None on site. Camping is available at Lake Simtustus, Cove Palisades State Park, Central Oregon KOA, Hay Stack Reservoir, and Jefferson County Fairgrounds. Lodging can be found in Madras.
Special attractions: Madras Pow-Wow; Journey Through Time Scenic Byway
Finding the site: Traveling from US 26 in Madras, take US 97 east for approximately 15 miles. Follow the sign to Ashwood, leading down Ashwood Road. After about 9 miles you will see the big polka-dot trailer where you will take a right and check in. The beds are 0.2 mile ahead.

Rockhounding

The famous Priday Polka-Dot Agate Beds are a fee-dig operation owned by West Coast Mining. The beds are generally only open from Memorial Day to Labor Day. That being said, please plan ahead and contact the mine before visiting. Days of operation can and will change. If the gate is closed, then they are closed for the day. When they are open, you are welcome to dig your own material or you can just purchase pre-dug material weighing up to several hundred pounds from the piles.

A fine polished slab specimen of Priday Polka-Dot Agate. RICE NORTHWEST MUSEUM OF ROCKS AND MINERALS SPECIMEN

The agate here is as its name suggests: polka-dotted. The prized material has a sugary white-to-blue base color with black, brown, or red dots. There's also a beautiful blue agate called "Blue Ice." Some pieces have little brown "snowballs" inside them. The "Blue Ice" polishes well, but can easily turn an opaque white if left out in sunlight. Some of the agate found here can have red or brown jasper running through it as well. All of the agate found here is well worth the visit.

To dig, bring your hard-rock mining arsenal. Heavy hammers, gads, chisels, and wedges all come in handy here. To break out large chunks, locate a crack and hammer a wedge into it, and wait a bit. While you're waiting the crack will be getting bigger. Repeat these steps until the material starts coming loose. Don't forget your gloves and eye protection. You will also find lots of material lying around the pit that is worth picking up or working over.

For pricing, availability, and more information about the mine, visit www.wcmining.com or contact West Coast Mining, PO Box 133, College Place, WA, 99324; (509) 522-4851. Their website also offers material for sale from their other claims in Oregon and locations in other states that are not open to the public.

26. Richardson's Rock Ranch

A beautiful cut and polished double thunderegg from the Blue Bed at Richardson's Rock Ranch.
RICE NORTHWEST MUSEUM OF ROCKS AND MINERALS SPECIMEN

See map on page 72.
Land type: High desert sagebrush
County: Jefferson
GPS: N44 43.955' / W120 58.557', 1,869 ft. (office)
Best season: Summer
Land manager: Private—Richardson's Recreational Ranch and Richardson Agate Co. LLC
Material: Agate thundereggs, opal thundereggs, jasper, agate
Tools: Geology pick, hammer, chisel
Vehicle: 4WD suggested
Accommodations: None on site; camping is available at Lake Simtustus, Cove Palisades State Park, Central Oregon KOA, Hay Stack Reservoir, and Jefferson County Fairgrounds; lodging in Madras

Special attractions: Madras Pow-Wow; Journey Through Time Scenic Byway
Finding the site: Traveling from US 26 in Madras, take US 97 east for approximately 11 miles; keep an eye out for milepost 81. On your right you will see signs for the ranch marking Old US 97. Travel this paved road for 1.8 miles. Turn right onto Hay Creek Road and drive about a mile and take a left to the office, another 0.3 mile ahead. Park here and check in.

Rockhounding

Many say, and I would agree, that you cannot call yourself a true Oregon rockhound until you have made the pilgrimage to the world famous Richardson's Recreational Ranch. Their land is home to some of the best thunderegg digging you can find anywhere in the world. First opened to the public in 1975, this well-organized and efficiently operated fee-dig site provides several thunderegg beds to dig from on their 17,000-acre operating cattle ranch. With the purchase of some neighboring land, they are now the proud owners and operators of the legendary Priday Plume and Kennedy agate beds. The Richardson family estimates that 65 percent of the thundereggs found on the market today were dug on their land.

There are agate thundereggs in seemingly infinite variations of color, inclusions, and sizes. Banding is the most common occurrence but inclusions such as moss and plumes in tones of red, yellow, and white can also occur.

Stop at the office at Richardson's and sign in if you want to dig thundereggs on their ranch. Look through the piles of rock when you are done digging, or you'll never make it to the pits.

Some eggs can have either hollow, crystal-filled geode centers or hollow centers with chalcedony stalactites. Many of the chalcedony-lined eggs fluoresce under short-wave UV light. There is a bed containing tiny light-blue opal-filled thundereggs. They are my personal favorite, even though some of them seem to craze a bit over time. Some of the opal is of facet grade. Other mineral attractions include a couple of fine jasper and agate beds.

To dig you need to first stop at the office/shop and register. The GPS coordinate listed is the shop parking lot. The Richardsons will provide you with an excellent map to the beds on their land and information on how to properly pluck out great material. If you don't have tools, they usually have some loaners. Expect a per pound fee and a per group minimum. A five-gallon bucket full of thundereggs is about fifty pounds, give or take. Call ahead to make sure the beds are open and save yourself a lot of gas and time. I've been turned away from digging due to wet weather.

The rock shop is open year-round and has many rocks from Oregon and around the world for sale. The shop also houses a small museum featuring local and regional minerals and fossils. A fantastic Chinese jade carving collection on display is the cherry on top. The Richardsons no longer provide on-site camping. The ranch can be contacted at 6683 NE Hay Creek Road, Madras, OR, 97741; (800) 433-2680; www.richardsonsrockranch.com.

27. Rooster Rock

Beautiful seams of blue banded agate can be found at Rooster Rock. Bring a good hammer and a chisel if you want to free them from their matrix.

Land type: Mountain forest hills and road cuts
County: Crook
GPS: N44 31.951' / W120 29.429', 4,432 ft.
Best season: Summer
Land manager: USFS—Ochoco National Forest
Material: Moss agate, agate
Tools: Geology pick, gad, chisel, shovel
Vehicle: 4WD suggested
Accommodations: Camping throughout Ochoco National Forest; lodging in Prineville
Special attractions: Stein's Pillar; John Day Fossil Beds: Painted Hills Unit
Finding the site: From Prineville or Mitchell, head to near milepost 49 and turn west onto NF 27. Follow the signs to the Lucky Strike Mine. After 1.3 miles you'll take a gravel road (NF 2730) to your right. Head down this progressively rougher road for about 6 miles to a fork in the road; stay to your left and continue along NF 2730 toward Lucky Strike. After another 3.2 miles you will come to another fork in the road. Continue along NF 2730 to your right. Lucky Strike Mine is to the left at this fork. From about a half mile down 2730 to about a half mile past the GPS reading you can find material. Drive about 1.0 mile to get to the tiny

Prineville

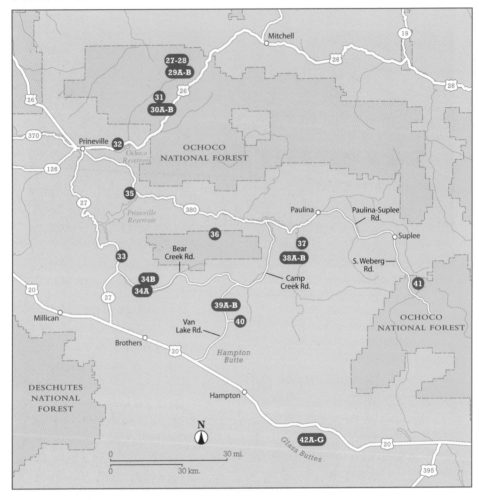

parking area on your right that is the GPS marking, or find a safe place to pull off on your own.

Rockhounding

The moss agate found in the Ochoco National Forest is second only to the material found at Maury Mountain. The area also hasn't been hit as hard, as the road leading in is not as inviting as the road leading to Maury. The roads in this part of the Ochoco National Forest can be snowed in until May. I was once back there in late March and got skunked by snow just about everywhere

Uncovering a moss agate seam at Rooster Rock.

I went. The terrain is also much steeper, so you'll want to be in good physical condition and have proper footwear before attempting to walk around the hills.

My GPS marking is a good place to pull safely off the narrow road and park. I found material from this point on to the top of the hill near the cattle guard to another half mile back down the hill. I wouldn't recommend bringing an RV to this site, as it would be too difficult to turn around. Material is found scattered everywhere throughout the hills from Rooster Rock all the way down to nearby Bear Creek, not to be confused with the Bear Creek (Site 34) south of Prineville with petrified wood. (There are a lot of Bear Creeks in Oregon and I imagine the rest of the country.) Search the hillsides for spots where you can find outcrops with veins of agate in the host rock to be worked out with hammers and gads. Chunks of agate are even lying in the middle of the gravel road. Do not be tempted to dig directly into the road, as not only can you get ticketed by the USFS for doing so, but it's just in bad taste to destroy the road.

Along with great green moss agate there is also plentiful banded agate in clear, gray, and blue tones and nodules sometimes with quartz crystals inside. The occasional piece of red jasper can be found as well. There is also potential for finding thundereggs throughout these hills, as well as the rest of this part of the Ochocos. Claims exist in the area, so watch out for markers. Tumbler-size material is abundant and as usual you'll need to do some serious searching or hard-rock mining for larger-size material.

28. Lucky Strike

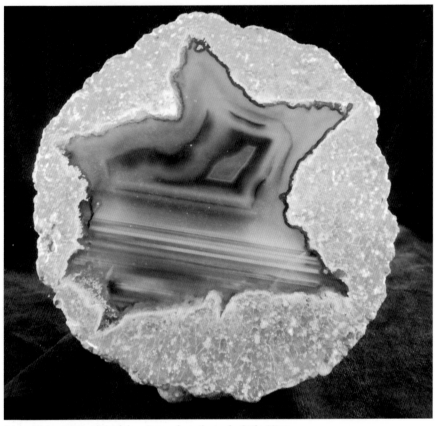

A beautiful cut and polished thunderegg from the Lucky Strike Mine.
RICE NORTHWEST MUSEUM OF ROCKS AND MINERALS SPECIMEN

See map on page 82.
Land type: Mountain hillside
County: Crook
GPS: N44 31.072' / W120 29.857'
Best season: Summer
Land manager: Private (mine); USFS—Ochoco National Forest
Material: Thundereggs
Tools: Pick, shovel

Vehicle: 4WD suggested

Accommodations: Primitive camping on site and throughout Ochoco National Forest; lodging in Prineville

Special attractions: Stein's Pillar; John Day Fossil Beds: Painted Hills Unit

Finding the site: From Prineville or Mitchell head to near milepost 49 and turn west onto NF 27. There will be signs from here on in to help guide you. After 1.3 miles, you'll take a gravel road (NF 2730) to your right. Head down this progressively rougher road for about 6 miles to a fork in the road; stay to your left and continue along NF 2730. After another 3.2 miles, you will come to another fork in the road. Take NF 200 to the left for 1.3 miles where you will find the well-marked entrance to the mine. It's another 0.3 mile to the shop where you park and check in. The mine can also be reached by continuing on NF 27, but the road is much rougher and narrower this way.

Rockhounding

The Lucky Strike mine is a fee-dig operation that was first discovered and claimed in the 1930s by mine owner and rockhound legend, Leonard "Kop" Kopinsky. The very productive hillside provides Oregon rockhounds with the opportunity to collect thundereggs with beautiful internal colors and patterns. Just about every color can be found inside Lucky Strike thundereggs, along with the occasional geode center containing botryoidal agate or quartz

The Lucky Strike Mine owners consistently scrape the walls of their claim, so rockhounds can always find fresh thundereggs.

crystals. Rarely the crystals can be amethyst. Many eggs also contain moss in a wide variety of colors. Sizes tend to run large and the mine owners regularly scrape the hillside with a backhoe, making sure that nobody walks away empty handed. The only minute downside to the Lucky Strike Mine is its accessibility. The road leading into the mine is long and bumpy, especially the last couple miles. This prevents many passenger cars and low-clearance vehicles from getting in. Other than the minor trouble getting in, the Lucky Strike Mine is one of Oregon's top thunderegg collecting sites and should be on every rockhound's checklist.

When you arrive at the mine, park at the shop and check in. If you're lucky, Kop will be there and he will tell you some of the best rockhounding stories you've ever heard. At the shop they have many examples of the material that can be found at their mine. From whole, cut and polished thundereggs to gorgeous finished cabochons, the variety is stunning. If you can drag yourself away from the great stories and beautiful material found at the shop, there's a lot of spectacular material just waiting for you to dig out for yourself. If you have your own favorite thunderegg digging tools, bring them. If you are without, the mine usually has some for loan. They will also direct you to which pits are currently the most productive and show you how to properly remove fresh, intact eggs.

Expect a per pound fee with a per group minimum. At the time of publication, the minimum was equivalent to ten pounds. Trust me, the minimum is very easy to obtain, especially when the pits are freshly scraped. My fellow rockhounds Chris and Sara Scheckla dug more than eighty pounds of large eggs in just a couple of hours when we visited in July 2012. The mine is typically open from May to October, weather permitting, and is closed on Tuesday and Wednesday. The Lucky Strike Mine can be contacted at PO Box 128, Mitchell, OR, 97750; (541) 462-3332.

29. Whistler Springs

Surveying the thunderegg pits at Whistler Springs for quality material.

See map on page 82.

Land type: Mountain forest

County: Crook

GPS: A: N44 29.802' / W120 29.166', 5,634 ft.; B: N44 29.764' / W120 29.117', 5,617 ft.

Best season: Summer

Land manager: USFS—Ochoco National Forest

Material: Thundereggs

Tools: Geology pick, hammer, chisel, gad, shovel

Vehicle: 4WD

Accommodations: Camping on site and throughout the Ochoco National Forest; lodging in Prineville

Special attractions: Stein's Pillar; John Day Fossil Beds: Painted Hills Unit

Finding the site: From Prineville or Mitchell take US 26 east to near milepost 49 and turn west onto NF 27. There will be signs from here on in to help guide you. After 1.3 miles, you'll take a gravel road (NF 2730) to your right. Head down this progressively rougher road for about 6 miles to a fork in the road; stay to your left and continue along NF 2730. After another 3.2 miles you will come to another fork in the road. Take NF 200 to the left and drive for about 6 miles to an intersection.

At about 1.3 miles along NF 200, you will pass the Lucky Strike Mine. You also will pass the Valley View Mine farther along. It is a private claim, so no collecting. At the intersection take a left, travel about 100 feet, and then take a right (southeast). You'll know you're on the right track when you see the Whistler Springs sign. Site A is located about 0.2 mile down this road near the outhouse and Site B just a few hundred yards farther down the road. Unless you have very high vehicle clearance, park at Site A near the outhouse and walk the short distance to Site B. Whistler Springs can also be reached by continuing on NF 27, but the road is much rougher and narrower this way.

Rockhounding

Whistler Springs has been set aside for recreational rockhound use and is featured on the *Central Oregon Rockhounding Map*. Agate thundereggs ranging from 2 to 5 inches are abundant and due to a rough road leading in, the site doesn't get hit as much as more popular sites. The Lucky Strike Mine is just a few miles away and can be distracting to visiting rockhounds. Even though the thundereggs found at Whistler Springs do not get as large as the eggs found at Lucky Strike, they are unique and usually full of agate. These eggs should provide plenty of interest to any thunderegg enthusiast.

Site A is located just below the outhouse. Look for pits made by previous rockhounds for a place to start digging. You should be able to find plenty of small eggs in the loose soil. The smallest eggs can be easily cut on a trim saw. Use a pick, gads, and a shovel to extract larger eggs from their home in the host rock.

Site B is just down the hill from the outhouse and offers another opportunity for digging. Back in the day there used to be more pits located even farther down the hill, but this area now lies within the Mill Creek Wilderness, where digging is not allowed. There is a fence marking the wilderness area to keep us rockhounds corralled in the right area.

There is decent primitive camping available on site and even a pit toilet making it easy to camp out for a few days and dig a ton of eggs. It would also make a good home base while exploring the many other sites found in this neck of the Ochoco National Forest. Keep in mind in this remote area the facilities don't get serviced very often. There were several presents left behind by resident rodents and no paper when I visited the site, so keep your expectations low.

30. White Fir

Jasper thunderegg from White Fir. Be prepared to dig for good eggs like this one.
RICE NORTHWEST MUSEUM OF ROCKS AND MINERALS SPECIMEN

See map on page 82.

Land type: Mountain forest

County: Crook

GPS: A: N44 24.478' / W120 33.399', 5,065 ft (main pits); B: N44 24.595' / W120 33.474', 5,152 ft. (more pits)

Best season: Summer

Land manager: BLM—Prineville

Material: Jasper thundereggs

Tools: Pick, hammer, gad, chisel, shovel

Vehicle: 4WD suggested

Accommodations: White Rock Campground; primitive camping throughout Ochoco National Forest; lodging in Prineville

Special attractions: Stein's Pillar; John Day Fossil Beds: Painted Hills Unit

Signs will help lead the way to White Fir Springs thunderegg beds. Funny it says AGATE BEDS even though they are jasper thundereggs.

Finding the site: Take US 26 (Ochoco Highway) from either Prineville or Mitchell. Drive to around milepost 41 and head north onto NF 3350. It's all gravel and dirt from here on in. At 0.4 mile you will come to a fork. To the right is a great campground. Follow the Agate Beds sign and continue to the left to reach the beds. Another 0.6 mile in you'll come to another fork. Again, stay to the left. Continue another 0.8 mile and you will come to yet another fork where you will be staying to the left. About 2.7 miles from this point you will pass a turn on the right to where the agate thundereggs are, but this spot is now claimed. From here continue another 0.3 mile and you will see another Agate Beds sign and a dirt road (NF 010) leading up the hill to your right. The beds (Site A) are another 0.1 mile down this road. To reach Site B, continue west along NF 3350 another 0.7 mile and take a very sharp turn onto NF 300. Drive 0.4 mile to a dirt road (NF 302) on your right. At this point look around for signs of digging and beds. A good parking area can be reached 0.1 mile down NF 302. At the end of NF 302 you can also find more thunderegg beds.

Rockhounding

This land has been set aside by the USFS for recreational rockhound use and is featured on the *Central Oregon Rockhounding Map*. Excellent camping sites are found nearby, making it easy to spend some time digging these unusual thundereggs. Pine trees can offer some welcome shade while digging in the hot sun.

It's been said that the jasper-filled thundereggs found here are some of the most beautiful jasper eggs in the world. You'd be hard pressed to find finer. The jasper inside can be found in shades of red, yellow, orange, tan, mauve, and burgundy. It is reminiscent of a type of jasper from Australia, known as mookaite on the mineral market.

On your drive in you will pass the White Fir Agate Thunderegg Beds. It has passed through many hands over the years but is now claimed by the Prineville Rockhound Pow-Wow Club. Clubs are allowed to dig with permission and only if they have insurance for their members. Otherwise it is off limits to collecting. The thundereggs here are agate filled with a green-toned rhyolite shell. There is also a lot of red jasper found at this site.

Site A is the main jasper thunderegg beds. It even has a sign. Site B is more of the same material. The method of attack is the same at each site. Look around for pits started by other rockhounds. This area has been a popular site for many decades and there are a lot of pits. Continue on these pits or start one of your own. The overburden is fairly soft and easy to dig. You will probably find eggs while digging in the dirt. Most of them will be duds, but you might find a few decent eggs. The best eggs are found in the hard rhyolite matrix found about 2 feet under the surface. Use hammers, chisels, and gads to free them from the host rock.

31. White Rock

Small thundereggs that can be cut on a trim saw are abundant at the T'N'T thunderegg bed near the White Rock Campground.

See map on page 82.

Land type: Mountain pine forest

County: Crook

GPS: N44 25.253' / W120 33.188', 5,327 ft.

Best season: Summer

Land manager: USFS—Ochoco National Forest

Material: Thundereggs

Tools: Pick, shovel, hammer, gad, chisel

Vehicle: 4WD recommended

Accommodations: White Rock Campground; camping throughout Ochoco National Forest; lodging in Prineville

Special attractions: Stein's Pillar; John Day Fossil Beds: Painted Hills Unit

Finding the site: Take US 26 from either Prineville or Mitchell. Drive to around milepost 41 and head north onto NF 3350. It's all gravel and dirt from here on in.

At 0.4 mile you will come to a fork. To the right is a great campground. Follow the Agate Beds sign and continue to the left to reach the beds. Another 0.6 mile in you'll come to another fork. Again, stay to the left. Continue another 0.8 mile to another fork where you will be staying to the left. After about 3.0 miles you will see another Agate Beds sign and a dirt road (NF 010) leading up the hill to your right. This is Site A for White Fir. To reach White Rock, continue west along NF 3350 another 0.7 mile and take a very sharp turn onto NF 300/Wildcat Mountain Road. The campground is at the end of the road about 1.8 miles in. Before the campground at about 1.3 miles, you will see a road (NF 350) on your left. There is a boundary fence about 0.1 mile down NF 350/Wildcat Mountain Lookout Road. The beds are just to the left of the fence. You can drive all the way in, but will have to back out, as there is nowhere to turn around. If you don't want to back out, park on NF 3350-300 and hike in from there.

Rockhounding

The digging area at White Rock runs right alongside of the Mill Creek Wilderness. Digging is not allowed on wilderness land. Luckily there's a fence to keep us rockhounds cordoned off in the right area with plenty of thundereggs to keep us all busy. This bed has been nicknamed the T'N'T bed, after the two rockhounds who first started digging a big hole in the bed; Tim Fisher and Terry Ensell. I wouldn't suggest trying to reach this site in wet weather.

The T'N'T thunderegg bed. Some of those rocks lying about are thundereggs.

Generally small (1- to 2-inch) yet abundant agate thundereggs are easily dug at this site. They are so small you have to use a trim saw to cut most of them. The agate is mostly clear to smoky colored. Some may even contain tiny quartz crystals. Occasional thundereggs with a purple staining on the quartz can be obtained, but they are not considered true amethyst, as it's just a staining and not in the crystal structure.

Digging at this site involves mostly pick and shovel work, but on the bright side, the dirt is relatively soft and easy to dig in. Look for loose eggs in the dirt. I like to use a screen to help find these. Some may still be lodged into chunks of rhyolite matrix. Bring a hammer to help free them. It shouldn't take you long to collect lots of these cute little thundereggs.

The campground at White Rock is an excellent place to stay for a few days while exploring the many Ochoco National Forest digging sites. There are two campsites with fire rings and a pit toilet. The campground provides access to hiking trails in the Mill Creek Wilderness area. The old White Rock thunderegg beds are located down this trail, but since they are now in wilderness area, digging is not allowed. They're now pretty much covered by pine needles anyway. If you know your mushrooms, keep an eye out for many varieties of fruiting mitochondria while rockhounding and camping in the area. Be aware that cougars live in these hills; their fresh footprints are occasionally found in soft dirt.

32. Ochoco Reservoir

Colorful jasper can be found throughout the hill at this site on the Ochoco Reservoir. Look for float, or try to locate an exposure high on the hill.

See map on page 82.

Land type: Steep treed hillside.

County: Crook

GPS: N44 18.357' / W120 42.431', 3,165 ft. (parking area)

Best season: Late spring–fall

Land manager: BLM—Prineville

Material: Jasper, agate

Tools: Geology pick, hammer, chisel, gad

Vehicle: Any

Accommodations: RV park and camping at Ochoco Reservoir; camping throughout Ochoco National Forest; lodging in Prineville

Special attraction: Stein's Pillar

Finding the site: From Prineville head east on US 26 to just before milepost 26. You'll take a left (north) onto a small unmarked gravel road. This is one of those turnoffs that are easy to miss, so keep your eyes peeled. If you miss it you can easily turn around at the nearby Ochoco Reservoir boat launch. Once on the gravel road, stay to your left; the road leading to the right is a private driveway.

A view of the Ochoco Reservoir from the collecting locality. You can also find material down there on the shoreline.

After just a few hundred feet you'll reach an open parking area. This is the GPS point I marked. From here you will hike straight up the hill to the north.

Rockhounding

This site is very close to the highway and is easily accessible by any vehicle. It makes a great spot to pull off while traveling the area, and once up the hill provides a stunning vista and photo opportunity of the Ochoco Reservoir. Collecting material entails mainly picking float up off the ground, but large pieces can also be worked out of outcrops farther up the hill. The challenge here is both finding large material and making it up the fairly steep hill. Be sure to be in good physical condition before hiking. The farther you can hike up, the better chance you'll have of finding an outcrop to work big chunks of jasper out of and generally larger pieces of float. Make sure to use eye protection if you choose this method of attack. The hill is also in a southern exposure, so avoid high heat times of the day and bring plenty of water.

Most of the plentiful jasper here is in red, green, and brown tones. Some of it contains veins of agate or pockets of small, sparkly druzy quartz crystals. Small agates can also be found. There is a nice layered brown variety dubbed Bat Cave Jasper also found scattered throughout the hillside. It's rumored that it comes out of a bat cave located high on the cliffs.

Locals say you can find pieces to collect in the Ochoco Reservoir at low water levels. I stopped by in July, and the water was low, but all the exposed rock was covered in some very stinky, dried, gross gunk. But it didn't prevent me from jumping in the water. It was a very hot day and I needed a bath. Maybe I should have been there in June for less dried gunk. I imagine there is potential for more material around the reservoir, which is only accessible by boat.

33. Fischer Canyon

A sample of agate, jasper, petrified wood, and calcite found at Fischer Canyon.

See map on page 82.

Land type: High desert sagebrush

County: Crook

GPS: N44 01.412' / W120 41.577', 3,650 ft. (fence parking area)

Best season: Late spring–summer

Land manager: BLM—Prineville

Material: Calcite, agate, quartz, jasper, petrified wood

Tool: Geology pick

Vehicle: High clearance on the dirt road

Accommodations: Primitive camping on site; slightly more developed camping along OR 27 near Prineville Reservoir; lodging in Prineville

Special attraction: Prineville Reservoir

Finding the site: From US 26 in Prineville take Main Street south where it will soon turn into OR 27. From town continue south for 30.7 miles. Take a left (east) onto an unmarked dirt road 0.1 mile south of Salt Creek Road. If you don't have high clearance, park here and hike the rest of the way in. At about 0.2 mile down the dirt road you will see places to pull off on both sides of the road. This is the beginning of the collecting area. You can continue up the road to the fence about 0.5 mile in. I usually park at the fence (GPS marking) and explore from there. From

Search the hills and ravines at Fischer Canyon for calcite, petrified wood, agate, jasper, and quartz crystals.

Bend use US 20 and take OR 27 north 14.1 miles to the dirt road on your right leading to the site. If you pass Salt Creek Road, you went about 0.1 mile too far.

Rockhounding

With the exception of calcite the other silicate minerals, minerals found at this site, are not abundant, but with its easy access and quality of material found, I decided to add this area to the book. It is also near the Bear Creek petrified wood location and offers the chance to collect more varieties of minerals while visiting the area. The area is featured on the *Central Oregon Rockhounding Map*. You can park at my GPS reading near the fence, or pretty much anywhere you want. You can cross the fence, but make sure to leave it as you found it. I had better luck searching north of the dirt road and east of the fence. Search for material throughout the hills, especially in dry washes and areas of accumulated rock. You will notice the large pit on the west side of the first large mesa north of the dirt road, though I'm still not sure what people were looking for there, as I found nothing.

The most common mineral at Fischer Canyon is calcite. It is clear to yellow-toned and nice naturally cleaved rhobohedral crystals can be found. The jasper is mostly red or green, and some can be brecciated. Pieces tend to be small tumbler material. With lots of searching and even more luck, some fist-size chunks can be obtained.

Though most of the agate found here tends to be small, it has a nice blue tint to it. I found some agate geodes on a hill east of the fence that had either calcite or quartz crystals in the center. One broken piece was about 3 inches by 3 inches, and had small quartz crystals with a very light amethyst tone. I can only wonder how much darker the amethyst could have been had it not been sitting in direct sunlight for however long.

Petrified wood found here is not common and tends to be porous, but some nice yet elusive solid pieces can be found. It mostly ranges in the brown and gray tones.

34. Bear Creek

Typical float petrified wood found at Bear Creek. Hold out for hard agatized material that will take a polish. Do some serious exploring or digging for large rounds.

See map on page 82.

Land type: High desert hills.

County: Crook

GPS: A: N43 56.450' / W120 37.161', 3,996 ft.; B: N43 57.927' / W120 37.161', 4,472 ft.

Best season: Late spring–fall; avoid wet weather

Land manager: BLM—Prineville

Material: Petrified wood

Tools: Pick, shovel

Vehicle: 4WD suggested especially for Site B

Accommodations: Primitive camping on site; developed camping along OR 27 north of the Prineville Reservoir boat launch; lodging in Prineville

Special attraction: Prineville Reservoir

Finding the site: From US 26 in Prineville take Main Street south. Main Street will turn into OR 27. Continue south for approximately 33 miles. The road turns to gravel at about 28 miles in. Take a left (east) onto Bear Creek Road. Don't take Little Bear Creek Road to the north. Travel 5.3 miles down Bear Creek Road where you will see a dirt road on your left (north). After 0.3 mile you'll reach a fence. Go

There are many spur roads worth exploring for petrified wood at Bear Creek. You'll need to get far away from the main digs for any decent float material.

through the fence and make sure to close it behind you. After the fence there is a fork in the road. Site A is to the right and Site B is to the left. To reach Site A take the road to the right and head 0.6 mile to the cul-de-sac and pits and park. The road to Site B is very rough and can be muddy when wet. Take a left at the aforementioned fork in the road. At 1.6 miles you'll hit another fork. When I was there it was marked by a sign posted to a juniper tree that had the initials JP on it. Take this fork to the left (north) another 1.4 miles to the next fork in the road marking Site B on a hillside. Park anywhere you can safely pull off the road in this area. Bear Creek Road is also easily accessible by taking OR 27 north from US 20.

Rockhounding

Bear Creek is one of many sites set aside by the BLM for recreational rockhound use and is featured on the *Central Oregon Rockhounding Map*. The petrified wood at this location exhibits good grain pattern and is highly prized by collectors. The wood quality can range from porous specimen quality to highly agatized pieces that take a wonderful polish. The lower-quality wood is mostly black, gray, and brown. Pieces with good agate replacement have the same color range, but can have some yellow coloring in them as well. Finding wood is not difficult at either of the sites listed. The challenge is finding large pieces. Logs weighing hundreds of pounds have been removed from this area, but are rare and not easily removed. Remember your petrified wood regulations. Small pieces of clear to blue agate, red jasper, and calcite can be found throughout the area as well.

Site A has been a popular rockhounding destination for generations. The float in this area has pretty much been picked dry over the years. The only way to find sizeable pieces is to dig a hole. Luckily the dirt is soft and easy to pick and shovel. Hike around the area and find evidence of previous digging and inspect the wood chips lying around to determine the quality of what was coming out of the hole. You can also try your luck at digging in any random spot. Whichever way you choose, just be sure to dig deep. The overburden here can be up to 4 feet. Many large pits were filled in by the BLM in the 1990s, but rockhounds made quick work of adding new ones. Don't waste your time digging directly where a large pit has obviously been filled in. You'll have a better chance of finding good material digging around the edge of it.

The road to Site B is a long, rough and bumpy drive. Be prepared before attempting to take it on; I blew a tire on the return drive after collecting. That being said, a rough road keeps many people out and therefore yields a better float collecting opportunity. There are also not many pits dug in the area yet, increasing the potential of finding big material. Find the few pits that have been dug and continue on them, or start one of your own.

35. Eagle Rock

A cut and polished slab of elusive Eagle Rock plume agate. Approximately 3.5 inches.
Rice Northwest Museum of Rocks and Minerals specimen

See map on page 82.
Land type: High desert ridge top
County: Crook
GPS: N44 11.116' / W120 40.141', 4,288 ft.
Best season: Late spring–fall
Land manager: BLM—Prineville
Material: Agate, jasper
Tools: Hammer, chisel, gad
Vehicle: 4WD suggested
Accommodations: None on site; camping in nearby Ochoco National Forest; lodging in Prineville
Special attractions: Antelope Reservoir; Post, Oregon (the middle-most part of Oregon)
Finding the site: Head west from Prineville on Combs Flat Road, which turns into Post-Paulina Road (OR 380). At 14.5 miles you will see a large rock on the right side of the road and a gravel road just past it on the right as well. Take this road, go across

the cattle guard, and head left. Travel about 1.0 mile to a fork. Take it to the right and travel 0.4 mile to another fork. Take a left and park at the bottom of the hill. Hike up the road to the fence, about 0.2 mile. From here hike up the steep hill about 0.3 mile to a fork where you'll take a left, continuing 0.1 mile up the hill to the collection area.

Rockhounding

Good material here is very scarce, but the quality of a nice piece of Eagle Rock plume agate keeps rockhounds returning to the steep hills to try their luck. Be in good physical condition and prepared to attack the very steep hill leading to the collecting area. Fluids are essential, especially during the summer months. You'll be looking at a 1.2-mile roundtrip hike. At one time in the past you could drive all the way up, but the BLM has since blocked the road.

This site has been set aside for recreational rockhound use and is featured on the *Central Oregon Rockhounding Map*. The ultimate prize here is the black or brown plume agate, but moss, dendritic, and botryoidal agate can be found as well. There is some interesting banded red-brown jasper around.

Eagle Rock has been hit hard over the years and is currently in need of some serious work. Material is still available, but it's a lot of hard work to remove any from the cliff faces. There are a lot of dangerous overhangs of vesicular basalt in potentially productive areas. I wouldn't recommend digging underneath them. Stick to areas with little overhang, pits, and especially float collecting. Some small but decent pieces can still be found littered throughout the hillside.

Look for this prominent landmark, known as Eagle Rock, next to the road leading uphill to the collecting area.

36. Maury Mountain

A cut and polished chunk of multicolored Maury Mountain moss agate.
RICE NORTHWEST MUSEUM OF ROCKS AND MINERALS SPECIMEN

See map on page 82.

Land type: High desert sagebrush

County: Crook

GPS: N44 04.677' / W120 20.869', 4,850 ft.

Best season: Spring–fall

Land manager: USFS—Ochoco National Forest

Material: Moss agate

Tools: Geology pick, hammer, chisel, shovel

Vehicle: Any

Accommodations: Camping throughout Ochoco National Forest; lodging in Prineville

Special attractions: Antelope Reservoir; Post, Oregon (the middle-most part of Oregon)

Finding the site: Head west from Prineville on Combs Flat Road, which turns into Post-Paulina Road (OR 380). On this road you will travel through the town of Post, which is the middle-most part of Oregon. After milepost 33 turn right (south) onto NF 16. The road will be gravel from here on in. You will cross a bridge and head 4.2 miles to a fork in the road. Take the road to the right (west) onto NF 1680 (Drake

The Maury Mountain agate beds. Signs will help lead you in.

Butte Road) and travel 0.9 mile to NF 1690 and take a right (west). Travel 0.8 mile and stay to your right to an open parking area. The digging area is the whole area down the hill from the parking area. The site is well marked and signs will help you along the whole way in.

Rockhounding

Maury Mountain is one of many sites set aside by the BLM for recreational rockhounding. The sagebrush hillside is host to beautiful moss agate in shades of brown, green, red, and yellow. Some of the agate here can also be banded or botryoidal. The roads, while mostly gravel and dirt, are well maintained and easy for any vehicle to travel. Almost anybody can dig at this great site.

This area has been known to rockhounds for decades, so be prepared to do some work for larger specimens. To get a hint on where to find the big stuff, walk around and locate an area where other people have been digging. Check the tailings for chips of quality material. Agate makes a distinct ping sound in contrast to other rocks when it comes in contact with a pick, gad, or shovel. It helps to keep your ears tuned in while digging.

For excellent tumbler-size material spend some time hiking around the large area. Even though this area has been hit for years, there always seems to be lots of float material lying around. Keep your eyes on the ground and just pick up agate. You should be able to find plenty of material to feed your tumbler at home.

The dirt here sticks to everything, especially the agate. In wet weather the dirt turns to mud and then sticks to you. A bucket of water and a small brush are especially handy for cleaning off any suspect specimens and your shoes. I was here once on a rainy October day and by the time I got back to my truck I was about 3 inches taller due to all the mud stuck to my boots.

If you stay overnight at the campgrounds near the dig site, take some time to hike the surrounding hills. You may find some large and interesting botryoidal agate chunks searching around the Maury Mountains area.

37. Congleton Hollow

This pink agate limb cast was just barely poking out of the ground. Watch for icebergs at Congleton Hollow.

See map on page 82.

Land type: High desert hills; sagebrush and juniper trees

County: Crook

GPS: N44 03.095' / W120 01.334', 4,006 ft.

Best season: Summer

Land manager: BLM—Prineville

Material: Agate limb casts, opalized wood, petrified wood

Tools: Geology pick, shovel, pick, screen

Vehicle: 4WD

Accommodations: Primitive camping on site and throughout BLM land; lodging in Prineville

Special attractions: Antelope Reservoir; Post, Oregon (the middle-most part of Oregon)

Finding the site: To reach Congleton Hollow from Prineville, head west on Combs Flat Road, which turns into OR 380 (Post-Paulina Road). At milepost 51 take a right (south) onto Congleton Hollow Road. The road will be rough from here on in. The first 1.1 miles of Congleton Hollow Road is private land, but through travel is allowed. After that, it's mostly BLM land. About 3.8 miles from OR 380, you should notice a spur road on your left. This nasty little track shoots off to collecting areas. You can also continue down the main road to the bottom of the hill, where you will find a campground. Many people like to explore the ravine down here and have dug some pits. There will be a spur road leading back up the hill. Take this road up and explore any spur road connected to it. This entire area is worth searching and digging.

Rockhounding

Congleton Hollow and Dendrite Butte are both a part of my top ten places to rockhound in Oregon and are also featured on the *Central Oregon Rockhounding Map*. Although both sites have largely the same material and they are but a stone's throw away from each other, they have different points of access. Roads do connect the two, but private land and fences prevent shortcuts. Some rockhounds also tend to like one site over the other, so I have decided to list them separately. I won't try to sway you by revealing which side I like best. I think it all boils down to working hard and having a bit of luck. I'll leave it up to you to pick your favorite.

The GPS reading I give will get you into the heart of the collecting area. Just about any spur road from this point will get you to a productive spot. The

Explore the many bumpy spur roads at Congleton Hollow for agate limb casts.

roads leading into and around Congleton Hollow are very bumpy. They are much better than the roads at Dendrite Butte, but still have full faith in your vehicle before leaving the highway. I don't recommend driving any vehicle on these dirt roads in wet weather.

Congleton Hollow and Dendrite Butte both offer rockhounds the prospect of finding fantastic and highly sought after agate limb casts, found in shades of pink, green, and blue. The agate can be banded, botryoidal, or contain quartz crystal cavities. Rarely some of the banded casts can display what is called an iris effect when properly sliced. Many casts also encapsulate permineralized wood, or consist of partially permineralized wood themselves, with some containing inclusions of moss or dendrites. Most people hunting the area are looking for large round limbs completely replaced by agate and/or having interesting inclusions. The real prizes here are rare and exceptional agatized seeds and nuts, but don't get your hopes up. They are very uncommon.

Congleton Hollow is known for its pink casts, but any color may be found. Most of the casts found will be chips or very small. Once you start finding better material, you'll start getting picky. Hike around to surface collect or dig a hole and screen the dirt. Get far away from the road for the best surface collecting. Cover as much area as you can and inspect everything, as many of the large casts I've found are icebergs and may be showing very little on the surface. There doesn't seem to be any rhyme or reason to where the casts will be. Hike around and look for accumulations of agate. This is also a good way to determine a potentially good spot to put a shovel in and dig a hole. Ravines and dry washes are generally good places to check too.

Opalized wood displaying well-defined growth ring replacement can be found throughout the sagebrush hills as well. The color ranges in varying tones of black, gray, and brown. Most of the opalized wood material is small broken chunks, but some large pieces can be found. It takes a good polish in a tumbler.

38. Dendrite Butte

A rare agate walnut cast, found near Dendrite Butte.

See map on page 82.

Land type: High desert hills; sagebrush and juniper trees

County: Crook

GPS: A: N44 01.356' / W120 03.525', 4,457 ft.; B: N44 00.620' / W120 03.807', 4,661 ft.

Best season: Summer

Land manager: BLM—Prineville

Material: Agate limb casts, opalized wood, petrified wood

Tools: Geology pick, shovel, pick, screen

Vehicle: 4WD

Accommodations: Primitive camping on site and throughout BLM land; lodging in Prineville

Special attractions: Antelope Reservoir; Post, Oregon (the middle-most part of Oregon)

Finding the site: Dendrite Butte is accessible from both OR 380 and US 20. From Prineville, on OR 380, travel to just after milepost 44. Take a right (south) onto Camp Creek Road. Drive 9.3 miles to a dirt road on the left (east). This is FR 6574; the first few miles are private land and BLM access is allowed. There should be a sign. The roads leading in are all very rough. Drive 1.9 miles till you reach a fork in the road. Take the fork to the left and travel another 1.7 miles to another fork and keep to the right. Drive 0.5 mile to yet another fork. From here you have options. Take it to the left and travel 1.1 miles to the pits at Site A. To reach Site B take the fork to the right and drive about 1 mile to a stock pond. You can park here and begin your explorations.

True Oregonians use umbrellas for sun, not rain! Searching for agate limb casts at Site B.

Rockhounding

Congleton Hollow and Dendrite Butte are two of my top ten places to rock-hound in Oregon and are also featured on the *Central Oregon Rockhounding Map*. Although both sites have largely the same material and they are but a stone's throw away from each other, they have different points of access. Roads do connect the two, but private land and fences prevent shortcuts. Some rockhounds also tend to like one site over the other, so I have decided to list them separately. I won't try to sway you by revealing which side I like best. I think it all boils down to working hard and having a bit of luck. I'll leave it up to you to pick your favorite.

The roads leading into Dendrite Butte are a bit nastier than those found at Congleton Hollow. I definitely wouldn't recommend trying to get an RV anywhere back there. The last stretch to Site B is especially nasty. Have full faith in your vehicle before you leave the pavement and have plenty of supplies on hand. That being said, the nasty roads keep some people out. While I have rarely ever seen any other rockhounds while hunting at this site, I do commonly see feral horses running around.

I'm not going to tell you exactly where, but I found an agatized walnut cast while hunting in this area. Don't get your hopes up too high, because they are very rare. The two sites given here are just two places you can begin a fruitful hunt. Just like at Congleton Hollow, hike around and hunt for float, or dig and screen. Either way is hot and dehydrating, so be sure to bring plenty of water. Dendrite Butte is known for having agate casts with black dendrites. These dendrites can be exposed more with careful grinding and polishing.

In 2012, my friends and fellow rockhounds Nate and Tammie Macalevy dug some huge holes in the area. Their efforts were rewarded with a giant opalized log. They also found some gorgeous red petrified wood reminiscent of what is found in Arizona. These hills can be a prosperous area for human backhoes.

39. Smokey Butte

Search the juniper and sagebrush hills near Smokey Butte for good float material to feed your tumbler with.

See map on page 82.

Land type: High desert sagebrush and juniper hills

County: Crook

GPS: A: N43 53.443' / W120 18.793', 4,718 ft.; B: N43 54.002' / W120 19.023', 4,539 ft.

Best season: Summer

Land manager: BLM—Prineville

Material: Jasper, agate, moss agate, petrified wood, agate and jasper limb casts

Tools: Geology pick, pick, shovel, screen

Vehicle: Most if you stay on the gravel roads; 4WD suggested if you get onto dirt roads

Accommodations: Camping on BLM land; lodging in Prineville

Special attractions: Antelope Reservoir; Post, Oregon, the middle-most point in Oregon

Finding the site: From Bend or Burns take US 20 to around milepost 54 and turn north onto Van Lake Road. Drive 13.1 miles until you see a dirt road on your left (west). Take this road and park at the intersection about 250 feet ahead. This is Site

The beginning of the collecting area designated as Site B. Make sure to do plenty of exploring on spur roads.

A and is where I made my GPS reading. Site B is another 0.6 mile north and is also a dirt road leading to the west. Take this road and try to find a good place to park. My second GPS reading was taken about 0.4 mile in and was a productive place to start.

From US 26 in Prineville take Combs Flat Road, which turns into Post-Paulina Road (OR 380). On this road you will travel through the town of Post, which is the middle-most part of Oregon. Between mileposts 43 and 44 take a right (south) onto Camp Creek Road. Drive 16.8 miles to the junction with Van Lake Road. Take Van Lake and continue another 5.7 miles until you see a dirt road on your right heading to the west. Take this road and try to find a good place to park. This is Site B. My GPS reading was taken about 0.4 mile in and was a productive place to start. Site A is another 0.6 mile south off Van Lake Road and is also a dirt road leading to the west. Take this road and park at the intersection about 250 feet ahead.

Rockhounding

This collecting area is like Hampton Butte, Maury Mountain, and Congleton Hollow/Dendrite Butte all combined together. This makes sense as Smokey Butte is very close to all of them. It's also very close to the well-maintained gravel road and is easily accessible to most vehicles. Both sites have similar material. I will say that when I visited I found much more float material at

Site A. I didn't find as much float at Site B, but I did find larger pieces for my efforts.

There is abundant and very bright jasper in almost every color at these sites. Some pieces are jasper-replaced wood casts similar to those found at Hampton Butte. Agates, with blue or pink hues, some with banding, are also very common. Some red and yellow moss agate can be found as well, but aren't as common. Rare agate or jasper limb casts can be obtained. The agate casts I found were small and of low quality, but you may be luckier. I did find a large jasper limb cast at Site B, but most material was very small. The petrified wood is also rare, but highly silicified for the most part, has good cell replacement, and will take a great polish. With all the material, lots of tumbler fodder can be picked up, plus the occasional slabable chunks.

This area is not well known to rockhounds, therefore material is still fairly abundant and the surface collecting is still very prosperous, for now. When I was in the area, there was very little evidence of digging, but putting a pick and shovel into the ground and screening for material could prove to be a fruitful endeavor. Take some time and do some more searching around the surrounding area. This part of Oregon is chock-full of minerals and you never know what you may find. Take care where you are hunting, because there is private land in the vicinity. Most of it is marked by fences and NO TRESPASSING signs to assist you from stumbling onto it, but it's always a good idea to have an up to date BLM map with you.

40. Hampton Butte

Petrified wood is found in a wide variety of colors at Hampton Butte. Bring a stiff brush and water to wash suspect specimens.

See map on page 82.

Land type: High desert, old growth juniper forest

County: Crook

GPS: N43 51.413' / W120 15.430', 4,773 ft.

Best season: Summer

Land manager: BLM—Prineville

Material: Petrified wood, jasper limb casts, agate limb casts, agate, jasper

Tools: Geology pick, pick, shovel, screen

Vehicle: 4WD suggested

Accommodations: Primitive camping on site; lodging in Prineville

Special attraction: Antelope Reservoir

Finding the site: From Bend take US 20 east for milepost 54 and turn left (north) onto Van Lake Road. Continue 10.6 miles then turn right (east) onto Price Twelve-Mile Road. This road is impassable when wet. Don't even try. After 2.2 miles you will begin to see dirt roads for the next 0.4 mile on your left (north) heading into an old growth juniper forest. These roads lead to the main collecting sites. There is also a road in that stretch headed due south that leads to more collecting. Once you pick a road to take, in a very short distance you will begin to see where people have been digging. Find a place to pull off and begin your search. My GPS reading was in the middle of some major pits.

Rockhounding

This is one of my top ten favorite places to be in Oregon. For one reason or another, the sunsets here are some of the most beautiful I've ever seen. The rockhounding is nothing to shake a stick at either. Hampton Butte boasts a rare green petrified wood. Wood also appears in many other colors such as brown, black, gray, and red. The fossil wood ranges from jasper casts to excellent cellular replacement displaying fine growth rings. The occasional agate limb cast can also be obtained. Agate and jasper are common. The agate can have some strange red moss-like inclusions and the jasper can be found in almost any color of the rainbow. The material here is from the famous Clarno Formation, which hosts many premier Oregon digging sites. Woods that have been identified are species closely related to modern day bald cypress, laurel, magnolia, oak, pine, sequoia, and sycamore.

Digging a hole for green petrified wood at Hampton Butte. Digging or searching through others' tailings are your best bet here.

Material can be found on both sides of Price Twelve-Mile Road. Do not cross fences, as they mark private land. Specimens can be obtained by hiking and collecting float or by digging in the relatively soft soil. Float collecting can be very prosperous for tumbling material and smaller pieces of wood, but you're probably not going to find logs or large limbs this way. Search the ravines and gullies for float when hiking around and be sure to check out people's tailings. Folks sometimes miss excellent pieces while digging, or the material just wasn't the size they were looking for. Out of curiosity once, I screened through someone's large tailings pile. They were probably looking for large logs and from the look of the pit, they must have been onto something. In a short amount of time screening, I was rewarded with half a five-gallon bucket full of great tumbling material.

For the big limbs, logs, and cutting material you're going to have to dig with a pick and shovel. There's no rhyme or reason to where material is lying underground. It could be anywhere. Sometimes you hit paydirt; sometimes you just dig a hole. Luckily the overburden is only about 2 feet thick so you don't have to dig too deep to get at good material. You can start your own pit, or continue digging out someone else's. If you're looking for big stuff and big stuff only, keep on digging until you find it. If you're like me, and you don't want to leave anything behind, bring a screen and sift through the dirt you dig out of your pit. The dirt here really sticks to buried material, so a bucket of water or sprayer helps identify choice material. There's a lot of porous green and red junk rock that can trick you into thinking it may be jasper. A good wash helps alleviate this problem.

41. Delintment Lake

Ammonites collected from the road cut at Delintment Lake.

See map on page 82.

Land type: Forested road cuts
County: Harney
GPS: N43 57.020' / W119 35.112', 5,630 ft.
Best season: Late spring–fall
Land manager: USFS—Wallowa-Whitman National Forest
Material: Ammonite fossils
Tools: Geology pick, chisel, packing materials
Vehicle: 4WD suggested
Accommodations: Delintment Lake Campground
Special attraction: Delintment Lake
Finding the site: From Prineville, take OR 380 (Post-Paulina Highway) for 72.8 miles (the road will turn into Paulina Suplee Road about 55 miles in) to S. Weberg Road. Take a right and drive 7.8 miles to NF 41. Take a right onto NF 41 and drive 3.8 miles to NF 43. Take a left onto NF 43 and drive just over 0.2 mile to a big road cut on your right. This is the site. This site is also accessible from Burns using NF 47.

Rockhounding

The sandstone deposits near Delintment Lake provide Oregon fossil hunters the opportunity to find interesting ammonite fossils and casts. Ammonites are

Prying fresh material out of the road cut at Delintment Lake. Be careful, that rock is sharp and pokey on the old behind.

a type of extinct cephalopod closely related to the modern day nautilus. Their spiral shells are a great example of logarithmic spiral or "the marvelous spiral" (nerdy math stuff). The ammonites here are a part of the Snowshoe Formation, which happened during the Jurassic Period.

The site recommended here is a good place to get started with your hunt and tune your eye. Get an idea of what you are looking for and then do some exploring in the area to find more sandstone exposures. There is a lot of private land in the area, so be respectful of the property owner's rights. Private land is generally marked and behind fences. Look for evidence of previous digging by other fossil hunters. Look for chunks of missing hill. Another good sign is a debris trail leading down a talus-covered hillside. These trails quite often lead uphill to a place where someone was once digging before.

Bring some paper towels and small boxes to wrap and house your collection until you get back home. The enamel on these shells will deteriorate, so if you want to save them you will need to add some sort of coating such as PaleoBOND. There are lots of websites with information on products that will help preserve your rocks.

Delintment Lake itself is a great place to camp, fish, and hunt. There is a fee campground with lots of sites, a boat launch, and a few pit toilets. If you are in the area during hunting season, be sure to bring and wear your bright orange colors.

For more details on fossil hunting near Delintment Lake, try to find the episode of *Oregon Field Guide* (KOPB) where they visit and dig with the National American Research Group at this site. Hook up with NARG if you really want to get into it. Tim Fisher's *Ore Rock On* DVD also has a lot of spots in this area marked, so you might want to check that out if you want to get serious with your fossil hunt.

42. Little Glass Butte

Break off corners of suspect obsidian to determine its quality. Here is a nice piece from the aurora borealis pit at Little Glass Butte.

Land type: High desert sagebrush

County: Deschutes

GPS: A: N43 34.185' / W119 58.664', 4,597 ft. (purple sheen); B: N43 33.163' / W119 59.539', 4,902 ft. (gold sheen); C: N43 32.948' / W119 58.569', 5,066 ft. (midnight lace); D: N43 32.581' / W120 01.079', 4,764 ft. (aurora borealis); E: N43 31.746' / W120 02.304', 5,195 ft. (leopard skin); F: N43 30.874' / W120 00.086', 5,052 ft. (red); G: N43 31.417' / W119 59.336', 5,552 ft. (rainbow)

Best season: Spring–fall

Land manager: BLM—Prineville

Material: Obsidian

Tools: Geology pick, pick, hammer, gad, pry bar, shovel

Vehicle: 4WD suggested

Accommodations: Primitive camping on site; camping/RV sites at Chickahominy Reservoir

Special attraction: Chickahominy Reservoir

Finding the site: Traveling east from Bend or west from Burns on US 20, head to just west of milepost 77. You will find a dirt road headed to the south. This is

Little Glass Butte

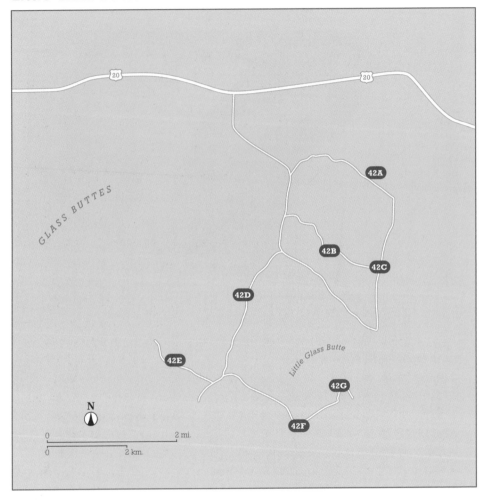

Obsidian Road, but the sign is long gone. Take this road and travel 1.7 miles to a dirt road leading toward the northeast and Site A (purple). Take this road 1.4 miles to some tracks on your left. Take these tracks 0.1 mile to the purple sheen pits. Site B is reached by continuing along Obsidian Road another 0.5 mile, from the turn for Site A, to a road on your left, leading to the east. Take this road 0.9 mile to an intersection and park. Gold sheen is common in this area. To reach Site C (midnight lace), take the same road as Site B, but travel about 1.9 miles east from Obsidian Road (or about a mile east of Site B) until you reach the large pits. If you

Inspecting the colorful obsidian of the aurora borealis pit. Little Glass Butte sits at the horizon.

hit a fence, you went too far. To reach the aurora borealis pits (Site D), drive past the turn for Sites B and C on Obsidian Road and continue 0.6 mile to a right turn by a large stock pond. Take the road to the right and drive another 0.9 mile to a road on the right. Head up this road just a couple hundred feet to a turnout near a tree on the right side of the road and park. The pits are across the road from here. Sites E, F, and G are found by continuing along the road past the turn for Site D another 1.2 miles to a road on your left. Taking this road will take you to Sites F and G. To reach Site E (leopard skin) continue along the main road for another 0.2 mile to a fork. Take the fork to the right and drive 0.6 mile to a steep road on your right. This hill is where the leopard skin obsidian is found. Sites F and G are very difficult to get to. The road is very rough and very steep. To reach them take the left off the main road and head up the hill. At about 2 miles you will reach a pullout to the right and Site F (red obsidian). Continue up the hill to reach Site G (rainbow), a total of 2.5 miles from where you turned off the main road.

Rockhounding

If obsidian is what your dreams are made of, then Glass Buttes is a dream come true. In the public collecting area on and around Little Glass Butte you will find high-grade material everywhere. The butte and the surrounding hills are literally made of obsidian. The biggest obstacle here is deciding on what color you want. Luckily you can camp at the site and collect them all, if you feel so inclined. The area brags many varieties such as black, mahogany, green, gold and silver sheen, leopard skin, rainbow, midnight lace, purple, and much, much more. The GPS coordinates provide just a few good places to get started. Fisher's DVD has coordinates for just about every pit located at Little Glass Butte.

To obtain material there are two forms of attack. First, you can hike the butte and hills and pick up plentiful float material scattered about. This is a great way to get small, roughly weathered cobbles that polish well when carefully tumbled. You can also find larger pieces this way. If you want a better chance at larger pieces, you will need to dig in a pit or start your own. Again, the biggest obstacle is choosing a color. Once you find the pit containing the obsidian you want, start prying it out. Use pry bars and gads in seams to separate material from the earth. To get an idea of the quality of color, use a geology pick or hammer to chip a small piece off the edge.

A final few words of caution; obsidian is *VERY* sharp. There's a reason indigenous people used this material for spear and arrowheads. Eye surgeons once used obsidian scalpels until the FDA banned the practice. The volcanic glass will have no trouble puncturing a tire, let alone cutting through flesh. Before you drive into this site, have full faith in your tires, a good spare tire, and maybe some fix-a-flat just in case. Wear gloves and especially eye protection if you plan on working a pit or when cleaving pieces of obsidian to check for quality.

43. Arbuckle Mountain

A sample of leaf fossils found at Arbuckle Mountain. Be prepared to break a lot of rock for good material.

Land type: Forested road cuts
County: Morrow
GPS: N45 12.979' / W119 15.563', 4,862 ft.
Best season: Late spring–fall
Land manager: USFS—Umatilla National Forest
Material: Leaf fossils
Tools: Geology pick, chisel, pry bar
Vehicle: 4WD suggested
Accommodations: Camping throughout Umatilla National Forest; Cutsforth State Park
Special attraction: McKay Creek National Wildlife Refuge
Finding the site: This site can be reached from a couple different directions. From US 395 in Ukiah take NF 053 west for approximately 14.8 miles to NF 5326 where you take it to the right. Drive 4.1 miles to NF 050. Take a right and travel 1.1 miles to the site. You will see pits at and near the curve in the road.

From OR 206, OR 207, and OR 74 near Heppner, travel just about a mile south of Heppner on OR 206/OR 207 to Willow Creek Road. Take Willow Creek Road east for about 16.8 miles and then take a slight left onto Black Mountain Lane.

Umatilla National Forest

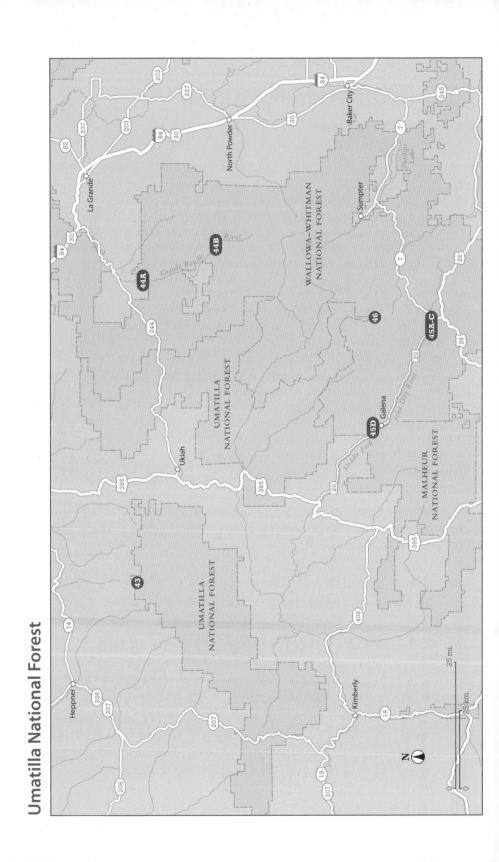

This road cut is a great place to start your leaf fossil hunt and tune your eye. Start your hunt where others have started. PHOTO BY SALLY FRANKLIN

Continue another 4.1 miles to NF 042 and take a left. Drive 0.2 mile to NF 050 and continue about 0.7 mile to a curve in the road that landmarks the site.

Rockhounding

The hills surrounding Arbuckle Mountain in the Umatilla National Forest are a spectacular place to do some leaf fossil hunting. Common plant species that may be found at Arbuckle Mountain include but are not limited to palm, willow, magnolia, laurel, oak, poplar, fern, and cypress. The palm leaves found in the area can be up to a couple feet long. Removing and lugging home whole specimens of the palms can be quite the challenge. Make sure you are equipped with tools such as heavy hammers, chisels, and pry bars.

There are many fossiliferous outcrops in the vicinity for fossil collectors to discover. The site listed here is a great place to get started and tune your eye. It will be quite obvious where people have been digging before. Remove chunks of rock and start splitting them. If you're lucky you'll expose leaves. Try to look for dark layers in the host rock. There are fossils in these layers. You want to try your best to split them using a heavy hammer and chisel, hopefully exposing the leaves in an aesthetically pleasing manner. Once you have an eye for things, get in your vehicle, do some exploring, and see if you can't locate something astounding.

When you visit this site, be sure to leave the site in better condition than you found it. Most of the local fossil-bearing outcrops are right next to the forest roads. Do not leave debris in the road under any circumstances. Even if you didn't make the mess, be a steward of good rockhound manners and clean up the road. The USFS does not like it when there is rubble in the road, especially when it is human-made rubble. Let's keep this delightful collecting locality open for generations upon generations of fossil lovers.

44. Grande Ronde River—South

Agate, jasper, petrified wood, porphyry basalt, and schist found at Site A near the bridge.

See map on page 124.

Land type: Forested riverbank and mine tailings

County: Union

GPS: A: N45 12.484' / W118 23.705', 3,479 ft. (river pullout); B: N45 03.278' / W118 17.672', 4,618 ft. (mine tailings)

Best season: Late spring–fall

Land manager: USFS—Wallowa-Whitman National Forest

Material: Quartz, granite, schist, agate, jasper, petrified wood

Tool: Geology pick

Vehicle: 4WD suggested

Accommodations: Camping throughout Wallowa-Whitman National Forest

Special attraction: Camp Carson Mine

Finding the site: Using I-84 from either Pendleton or La Grande, take exit 252 for OR 244 (Hilgard Highway) toward Ukiah. Drive down OR 244 for approximately 12 miles until you meet up with NF 51 (Grande Ronde River Road). Take a left onto NF 51 and drive about 4.3 miles to a pullout on your right by the river. This is designated Site A. You will know you are getting close to this pullout when you enter national forest land. To reach Site B continue south on NF 51 for 8.3 miles where you will hit a fork.

Hunger for gold turned this stretch of the Grande Ronde River upside down. These tailings piles seem to run on forever and now feed rockhounds' appetites.

Stay to the left (NF 5125) and continue another 6.6 miles to a road on your right. This will be NF 5138. Turn here and just about everywhere you will see piles of rocks. Be sure to check out the Camp Carson sign on your way in.

Rockhounding

This area in the Wallowa-Whitman National Forest was at one time a booming gold mining district. The hydraulic mining operations basically flipped the valley floor upside down in search of the precious shiny metal. This type of mining practice wreaks havoc on the local environment. In recent years a lot of reclamation work has been done in the area and things are starting to look much better. On the drive to Site A, be sure to stop to check out the signs about the Camp Carson mining district and the reclamation.

Site A is just one of many pullouts that give access to the Grande Ronde River along NF 51 on your drive in to Camp Carson. This stretch of the river has the better agate in my opinion. My GPS mark was taken at a pullout just after you enter the national forest land heading south on NF 51. As you head south from here, watch closely for pullouts. Every one we checked had some sort of path leading down to the river. Sally found a nice big agate with some red bloodstone-like spots in it. We also found lots of colorful jaspers and a couple pieces of nice hard petrified wood.

Site B includes the tailings piles left behind by a not-so-distant mining past. They seem to stretch on forever. My GPS marking is just a place to get started. Drive the road until you feel you have found a pile worth exploring. The huge piles are full of quartz and granite. Much of the quartz is what you would call sugar-agate, and can be very colorful. Sugar-agate looks a lot like agate, but is much too grainy when a fresh face is exposed. The granite is classic salt and pepper. Sparkly schist is very common. Jasper in yellow and brown tones can be found as well.

45. Middle Fork John Day River

A slab-worthy piece of yellow jasper found at Site D, near the town of Galena.

See map on page 124.

Land type: River and creek beds

County: Grant

GPS: A: N44 35.609' / W118 30.695', 4,071 ft. (wormhole rock); B: N44 36.130' / W118 32.042', 4,040 ft. (Vinegar Creek); C: N44 36.545' / W118 32.659', 4,021 ft. (Vincent Creek); D: N44 42.891' / W118 32.659', 3,401 ft. (Middle Fork John Day River)

Best season: Summer–fall

Land manager: USFS—Wallowa-Whitman National Forest / Malheur National Forest

Material: Agate, jasper, petrified wood, wormhole rock

Tool: Geology pick (for prying)

Vehicle: Any

Accommodations: Developed and primitive camping along John Day River

Special attractions: Ritter Hot Springs; Journey Through Time Scenic Byway; Blue Mountain Scenic Byway; Elkhorn Drive Scenic Byway; Old West Scenic Bikeway

Finding the site: From US 26 take OR 7 1.1 miles north to CR 20 (Middle Fork Road; Old West Scenic Bikeway). Take a left onto CR 20 and drive 0.6 mile to Site A. Look for the turnouts near the road cut. Site B is reached by continuing along CR 20 1.3 miles from Site A. There will be a gravel road on your right. Turn onto it, park safely off the road, and find your way down to Vinegar Creek to collect. Site

The expansive tailings at Site D contain agate, jasper, and petrified wood.

C is another 0.7 mile along CR 20 from Site B. Either safely park on the shoulder on your left or take a right onto NF 646 and drive a few hundred yards to the fence and park. You will notice extensive gravel deposits to collect from. Site D is reached by continuing along CR 20 from Site C for another 18 miles. Find the pullout on your left, park, and begin searching the gravels.

Rockhounding

This area was once well worked for its gold deposits. The small community of Galena was first established as a mining camp called Susanville in 1865. The remnants of past gold mining are easily seen in the massive gravel tailings piles found throughout the area, especially around Elk Creek near Galena. Eerie old mine shafts and run-down buildings from past mining camps can be seen throughout the hills. There are still many active claims throughout the area, so look out for claim markers.

Today rockhounds can search for agate, jasper, and petrified wood in the gravels of the Middle Fork John Day River and its many tributaries. Site A has an interesting pumice-like rock dubbed "wormhole rock." It has no real lapidary use, but makes for a curious garden rock. The other GPS readings are places I found easy access to gravel deposits. Other points of river access can also be found if staying at nearby campgrounds.

The agate tends to be clear, some with iron staining. Sally found an agate similar in shape to the sacred rocks used in an Indiana Jones movie. It has been dubbed "kali-ma," and now resides on the dashboard of my truck. The jasper is mostly red and/or yellow and some pieces can have some small interesting swirls throughout them. Pieces big enough to slab can be found. The petrified wood is highly silicated and will take a great polish. It is found mostly in brown and gray tones.

46. Greenhorn

Petrified tempskya is extremely rare, but you will find lots of jasper in the Greenhorn tailings.

See map on page 124.

Land type: Forested mine tailings
County: Baker/Grant
GPS: N44 43.082' / W118 29.849', 6,194 ft.
Best season: Late spring–fall
Land manager: Private—collecting allowed by custom. Be on your best behavior.
Material: Quartz, agate, jasper, petrified tempskya wood
Tool: Geology pick
Vehicle: 4WD
Accommodations: None on site
Special attraction: Ghost town of Greenhorn
Finding the site: From either direction on US 26, find your way to Austin Junction. Turn north onto OR 7 (Whitney Highway) and drive about 11 miles to Greenhorn Road. You can also take a shortcut to Greenhorn Road using NF 1035, but this route is a little more bumpy. Take Greenhorn Road 10.3 miles and look for a dirt road on your right. Take this road to the gravel piles about 0.4 mile in.

These are the old tailing piles around Greenhorn that may contain the elusive and rare petrified tempskya.

Rockhounding

The area in and around the city/ghost town of Greenhorn was once long ago a very productive gold mining district. People still live there seasonally and mine gold to this day, although officially the population is zero. Greenhorn is currently Oregon's highest and smallest incorporated city. The legend of how Greenhorn received its name is interesting. The story goes that a couple of new miners (known as greenhorns) arrived in the area and asked a local where they should start digging. The person they asked pointed off in a random direction and said "over there." The fresh miners headed off "over there." Lo and behold, they just happened to find gold and strike it big. The area was then named Greenhorn.

These days the main material people are looking for around Greenhorn, besides gold, is the rare petrified tempskya. Once thriving in the Lower Cretaceous period, tempskya is now an extinct genus of tree-like fern. The living plant could grow up to almost 15 feet tall. Its "trunk" is actually a mass of stems and roots. The petrified version is found in brown-yellow to brown-red tones and takes an excellent polish.

I have heard from locals that nearby McNamee Gulch and Winterville Creek are also good places to search for the elusive tempskya wood, but I did not have time to verify their accessibility during our visit. If you have time and good maps, try to check out these areas for the elusive petrified tempskya. There is also lots of black and green serpentine in the area suitable for carving. Keep your eyes peeled for outcrops to search.

47. Coyote Point

Hike the hills of Coyote Point for specimens of the green copper mineral, malachite.

Land type: Sagebrush hillside
County: Baker
GPS: N44 55.398' / W117 54.688', 3,723 ft.
Best season: Spring–fall
Land manager: Private—open by custom to casual collecting. Be on your best rockhounding behavior. If you come across "keep out" signs or fences, then respect the owners' rights and stay out.
Material: Malachite, azurite, chrysocolla, calcite, granite
Tools: Geology pick, hammer, chisel, gad
Vehicle: 4WD suggested
Accommodations: None on site; camping, lodging, and RV parks in area
Special attraction: Eastern Oregon Museum in Haines
Finding the site: From I-84 near North Powder, use exit 285 and take US 30 south about 8.5 miles to Haines. From downtown Haines take 3rd Street east for 0.9 mile. Then take a left onto Haines Dump Road and drive 0.9 mile to Coyote Peak Road. Take a right and start looking for the dirt spur roads on your right;

East

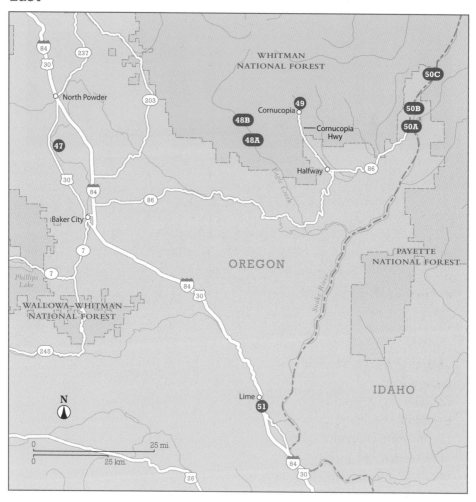

there should be three. They will all take you up the hill to a road running along the power lines heading south. From Coyote Peak Road it will be about a half mile to a set of ruts leading up the hill to the east. If you have a sturdy high-clearance rig you can take these ruts about 0.1 mile until they basically end. Note that it can be difficult to turn around once up here. Be a good reverse driver if you plan on taking this last stretch. If not try to pull off the road, park, and hike the rest of the way.

A view of historic Haines and the Blue Mountains, from the collecting area at Coyote Point.

Rockhounding

Nestled in the hills, just above the city of Haines, lies a copper deposit that has not been worked in many years. This spot offers a rare opportunity in Oregon to find bright green malachite, light blue chrysocolla, and even rarer dark blue azurite. Before you get your hopes up thinking of the excellent copper ores you may have seen coming out of the southwest United States or the Democratic Republic of the Congo, the material found at this site is not nearly as striking. It doesn't really have any lapidary use. Most of the malachite and other ores are like a thick staining on the brown host rock and calcite. Be picky and only bring home the best pieces you find.

The GPS I took here is a spot where you can work fresh material out of the hillside. Search the area mentioned here and also the surrounding hillsides for other pits and loose rocks showing evidence of green, light blue, and dark blue. Green stains will definitely be the most common. Take these rocks and smash them with a heavy hammer to try to expose fresh material. When you find a good chunk, you can try to cleave off as much of the host rock as you can, but the risk of smashing the whole thing into pieces is high. Over the years I've gotten fairly decent at trimming material with a geology pick, but I still destroy great pieces here and there. If you own or have access to a rock saw, you can also trim the matrix off.

An active granite quarry lies between the digging site and downtown Haines. For all you rock carvers, excellent specimens of granite can also be found throughout the hills near Coyote Peak. Be on the lookout for large salt and pepper material good enough to be worth lugging home.

48. Eagle Creek

Fossils found in the outcrop at Site B.

See map on page 133.

Land type: Forested road cuts

County: Baker

GPS: A: N44 56.606' / W117 19.994', 3,412 ft. (pullout); B: N44 59.071' / W117 22.287', 3,752 ft.

Best season: Late spring–fall

Land manager: Site A: USFS—Wallowa-Whitman National Forest; Site B: Private—open by custom to casual collecting. Be on your best rockhounding behavior. If you come across "keep out" signs or fences, then respect the owners' rights and stay out.

Material: Fossils

Tools: Geology pick, hammer, chisel

Vehicle: 4WD suggested

Accommodations: Camping available nearby

Special attraction: *Paint Your Wagon* movie site

Finding the site: You can reach this area a few different ways. I'm suggesting the way in that I prefer. You can also reach the site taking New Bridge Road to Eagle Creek Road north from Richland. From Baker City, take OR 86 east for about 23

One of the many limestone outcrops found along Eagle Creek. Please try to keep material out of the road, so we can keep enjoying this location.

miles to Sparta Lane. Take Sparta Lane north for 4.8 miles to a fork and take it to the left on E. Eagle Creek Road. Continue for 5.6 miles and take a right onto NF 7015 (Enterprise Gulch Road). Drive 4.6 miles down the hill to a bridge that meets up with NF 77. The pullout for Site A is to the right about 0.6 mile up the hill. You will pass the fossil-bearing outcrops on your way up the hill. From the bridge, Site B is to the left about 0.2 mile up NF 77 just past NF 7745. Look for a good pullout on your right. The big pile is the spot to dig.

Rockhounding

The limestone found near Eagle Creek in the Wallowa–Whitman National Forest provides the Oregon fossil hunter with many excellent outcrops full of marine fossils. Most commonly found here are fossil sponges, corals, and mollusks. There is also potential for something even bigger.

University of Oregon professor Dr. William Orr and his students first discovered ichthyosaur ribs and vertebra here in 1979, but it wasn't enough to identify the species. They needed a skull. Throughout the '80s they continued to find more ribs and vertebra, but no skull. About a decade later working for the Oregon Museum of Science and Industry (OMSI), Dr. Orr led a group of high school students to the site. A 15-year-old boy named Sam Jordan found a skull. The skull is what helped scientists identify the ichthyosaur as an Asian species known as "Shastasaur." Finding this skull has helped prove the theory that the Wallowa, Elkhorn, and Klamath Mountains were built of rocks that originated in the South Pacific as islands and coral reefs.

Now that I have you all pumped up about giant marine reptile fossils, I have to burst your bubble. If you find vertebrate bones here, you must report it to the USFS and get a permit if you want to dig more bones—but a permit is not an easy thing for the average fossil hunter to obtain. Everyday collectors like you and me will have to be happy with the fossils that don't have spines.

The sites listed here are two good limestone exposures. There are many more found throughout the area if you are up for some exploring. The limestone is mostly black to gray and pretty easy to identify. Once you have located an exposure, it's time to start breaking open some rock. I myself am not particularly adept at exposing whole fossils. I tend to break a lot of what was good material. Have lots of patience when trying to expose these delicate fossils. I suppose you have to break a few eggs to make an omelet. Bring paper towels and a small box to protect and transport your finds. Speaking of eggs, I should mention that people sometimes use egg cartons for transporting fossils.

A fun distraction while visiting the area is the movie site for the 1969 musical *Paint Your Wagon*. The movie is about two prospectors who marry the same woman in a "California" gold rush town. It stars Lee Marvin and Clint Eastwood and they both sing in it. If you haven't seen it, you must. The movie site is located about 3.7 miles up NF 7745 and is definitely worth a visit.

49. Cornucopia

Remnants of a not so distant mining past can still be found in Cornucopia.

See map on page 133.

Land type: Forested mine dumps and creek gravels

County: Baker

GPS: N45 00.745' / W117 12.869', 5,780 ft. (Union Mine)

Best season: Summer

Land manager: USFS—Wallowa-Whitman National Forest

Material: Quartz, granite, pyrite, epidote, porphyry basalt, schist, agate

Tool: Geology pick

Vehicle: 4WD suggested

Accommodations: Primitive camping on BLM land, McBride Campground; lodging in nearby towns

Special attractions: Historic Halfway; Cornucopia Ghost Town

Finding the site: From Baker City take OR 86 to the city of Halfway. Before town you will see an old burning silo and then a sort of intersection. Take the road to your left and drive about a mile into town. You will now be on the Cornucopia Highway. It's paved about halfway (nudge nudge), and then it turns to gravel and dirt. After the pavement ends there are decent pullouts with creek access. Just make sure you're not on private property. From town travel about 10.5 miles until you reach a fork. There is a Wi-Fi hotspot located here! To the right is the Cornucopia Lodge. Continue to the left. You will cross Pine Creek and head into Cornucopia. About a half mile

Large cobbles of quartz and granite pave the steep road leading up to the Union Mine in Cornucopia.

from the fork, you will reach a nasty rock and dirt road heading up the hill. About 1.4 miles up this rough bit of track is the Union Mine and mill ruins.

Rockhounding

Gold was first discovered in the Granite Mountains in 1870. Miners flocked to the region and the Cornucopia Mining District soon became one of the largest gold mining districts in America. From 1880 until 1941 the six mines produced more than 316,000 ounces of reported gold. In 1942 Roosevelt enacted Executive Order L-208, stating that all mining non-essential to the war effort be ceased. The mines all shut down, and although it's believed that there is a lot of gold still sitting in the old mines, the current owners have not tried to mine recently.

Although not much gold is coming out of the area these days, the mining history and rockhounding make the trip worth a visit. The Union Mine is reachable, but only by high-clearance 4WD vehicles. I made it about 0.2 mile up the road and had to stop and park. I hiked the rest of the way up to the mine, only to realize I had forgotten my camera back at the truck. Along the hike and at the mine I found tons of white quartz, salt and pepper granite, and pyrite.

For those rockhounds without a high-clearance beast-mobile, hunting Pine Creek is your best option. Find a good place along Pine Creek to pull out along the drive to the mine. There is a lot of private property in the area so be respectful of the land owners. I sampled a few spots and found lots of white quartz, salt and pepper granite, brassy pyrite, green epidote, sparkly schist, porphyry basalt, and a few teeny-tiny clear agates.

In the 1990s, during the dot-com boom, the nearby town of Halfway unofficially changed its name to Half.com, as a promotion for the website. On some maps it is still marked as Half.com with Halfway listed in parentheses. Halfway is the nearest place to the collecting sites for supplies. I like the place that is half Do-it Best hardware store and half grocery store.

50. Snake River (Homestead)

Samples of the red jasper and green epidote found at Site C.

See map on page 133.

Land type: River gravel bars, mine dumps

County: Baker

GPS: A: N44 58.420' / W116 51.310', 1,693 ft. (Copperfield Campground); B: N45 00.653' / W116 51.020', 1,756 ft. (copper mine dumps); C: N45 04.810' / W116 47.204', 1,702 ft.

Best season: Any

Land manager: BLM—Vale

Material: Pyrite, bornite, malachite, azurite, chrysocolla, native copper, galena, quartz, epidote, jasper, agate

Tools: Geology pick, hammer

Vehicle: 4WD suggested

Accommodations: Camping and RV parks along Snake River

Special attractions: Snake River; Hells Canyon Scenic Byway

Finding the site: Use OR 86 from Halfway or US 71 from Idaho to get to Oxbow. Site A is located here at the Copperfield Campground. To reach the rest of the sites, take Homestead Road north from the intersection near the campground and drive 2.8 miles to Site B. Site C is another 6.2 miles north at the end of the road.

A view of the picturesque Snake River running through Hells Canyon.

Rockhounding

The hills surrounding this area of the scenic Snake River are rich in copper minerals, silicates worth polishing, and other collectable minerals. The river is very popular with boaters and campers and can be quite packed during the summer months. Finding places to park can be iffy, but not at all impossible. Listed here are some areas I had success finding material. Be sure to explore any open pullout for river access and especially gravel deposits. There is a lot of private land in the area. Be respectful of the landowner's rights.

Site A is definitely the most accessible and therefore the hardest hit site here. The Copperfield Campground offers a day use area, tent camping, and RV hookups. If just visiting for the day, park in the well-shaded day use area and make your way down to the river. Search the gravel deposits for quartz, agate, jasper, and porphyry basalt.

Site B is the dumps of an old copper mine just above the Thorn Flats Campground. If the campground is not busy, just pull into the shaded area of an open campsite to park. If the place is packed, just park near the pit toilet. The dumps are located pretty much straight up the hill from the toilet about 50 yards. Bring a good hammer and start cracking rocks open. Look for pyrite, bornite, galena, native copper, malachite, azurite, and chrysocolla. Rocks with a blue to green stain on them are rich in copper and often worth busting open.

Site C is located at the very end of the road. The road is narrow and signs will warn you about having long loads. It's difficult to turn around or back up out here. Once you reach the campground area, try to park as far north as you can. The gravel deposit is just north of the camping area. Search the wash of Copper Creek for huge pieces of brick-red jasper, epidote, copper ores, porphyry basalt, and some small agates. There is private land to the west of this site. There are a fence and signs to keep us rockhounds out.

51. Lime

White orthoclase feldspar crystals found at the road cut in Lime.

See map on page 133.

Land type: Road cut

County: Baker

GPS: N44 24.040' / W117 18.370', 2,381 ft.

Best season: Any

Land manager: Private—collecting allowed by custom. Be on your best behavior.

Material: Orthoclase feldspar crystals

Tools: None

Vehicle: Any

Accommodations: None

Special attraction: Columbia River Gorge

Finding the site: This site is easily reached from I-84 at both Lime exits 342 and 345. From exit 342, take old US 30 (Oregon Trail Boulevard) south for approximately 1.4 miles. Just past the old cement plant, you will find a short pullout to park at on the east side of the road by the hill. From exit 345 the site is reached by taking old US 30 north for approximately 1.9 miles to the same pullout just before the old cement plant.

Rockhounding

The large road cut near the old cement plant in Lime provides Oregon rockhounds with the opportunity to collect small white orthoclase feldspar crystals. The material has no real lapidary use, and is of mostly specimen-collecting interest only. Still the white crystals are interesting enough to make this site a good place to collect. It also makes for a good place to stop and stretch your legs while traveling I-84 through eastern Oregon.

Search the talus slope for small white crystals both loose and in matrix. It takes a minute to tune your eyes, but once you start to identify them, they are very easy to spot. Hold out for especially nice feldspar crystals and crystals still in matrix. This spot has been hit for many years. Take only what you need and leave plenty of crystals behind for future generations of rockhounds to enjoy. Also be very careful not to knock loose material out into the road. That's a good way of getting a site shut down to collecting, plus it's just in bad taste to do so anyway.

This may not be a great place for kids and especially pets. The parking area is pretty small and you should be sure to pull well off the curvy road. The same word of caution goes for collecting. There's not much room between the hill and the road either. There's not much traffic through here, but other vehicles and semis are not going to expect you to be hanging out on the side of the road.

You can sift through the talus for orthoclase feldspar at the road cut in Lime.

52. Grande Ronde River—North

A sample of commonly found material collected at Grande Ronde River.

Land type: Riverbed gravels
County: Wallowa
GPS: A: N45 53.981' / W117 29.057', 1,731 ft.; B: N45 53.952' / W117 28.403', 1,723 ft.; C: N45 55.491' / W117 27.149', 1,630 ft.
Best season: Summer
Land manager: Oregon Department of State Lands (ODSL)
Material: Porphyry basalt, quartz, schist, jasper, agate
Tool: Geology pick
Vehicle: 4WD suggested
Accommodations: Camping along the Grande Ronde River; lodging in Troy
Special attraction: Rafting the Grande Ronde River
Finding the site: From La Grande, take OR 82 toward Elgin. About 26 miles past Elgin, start looking for Promise Road on your left. Take Promise Road 17.9 miles and take a right onto Wallupa Road. Drive 15.6 miles until you see a bridge. This is Site A. There are good pullouts and camping on either side of the bridge. From the other end of the bridge, continue east 0.6 mile to a boat launch/pit toilet. This is Site B. Continue east for 4 miles to a day use area on your right. This is Site C.

Coming from Enterprise, take OR 3 (Enterprise-Lewiston Highway) north for about 33 miles. Take a left onto Flora Lane and drive 2.8 miles to an intersection. Take a right and stay on Flora Lane for 0.4 mile. Take a left onto Lost Prairie Road and

Northeast

Site B at the Grande Ronde River. Look through the clean gravels for plentiful porphyry basalt and the occasional agate.

drive 2.9 miles to Redmond Grade Road and take a left. Drive 7.8 miles and then take a left onto Grande Ronde Road / Troy River Road. Drive 1.6 miles where the road will become Bartlett Road. Continue 0.4 mile until the road turns back into Troy Road. Site C will be another 2.2 miles down this road on your left.

Rockhounding

This northern stretch of the Grande Ronde River is a very popular spot with boaters and anglers. During our visit Sally and I saw several groups of people landing at the two boat launches found at Sites A and B. Many of the people we met there were surprised that we weren't out boating as well. After we explained to them we were there rockhounding, I noticed many of them started looking through the gravels themselves. I started wishing I could borrow one of their boats. It would have been nice to do some exploring on untouched gravel bars along the long Grande Ronde.

Sites A through C are all good spots to pull out with gravel access. Site A has a couple decent spots to set up camp and a rope swing under the bridge. There are a lot of ranches in the area that use the river and the livestock can muck up the water a bit. You will generally find that there are three levels of rocks on the river shoreline: green-brown slime covered rocks in and by the water, and then a layer of white crust covered rocks, followed by clean/dusty rocks. Look through the clean gravels to locate material.

The gravels contain an abundance of really good porphyry basalt (aka Chinese writing rock or chicken track basalt). Some of the intersecting feld-spar crystals in the basalt really do look like Asian logograms. Sizes range from tumbler material to large boulders good for decorator yard rock. The basalt will take a decent polish in a tumbler. White quartz is very common and will tumble well. On your explorations you can also expect to find sparkly schist, small bits of red to brown jasper, and a teeny-tiny clear agate here and there.

53. Imnaha River

The road leading into Site B is very bumpy, but with a vista like this, it is worth the drive to collect at the Imnaha River.

See map on page 145.

Land type: Forested riverbank

County: Wallowa

GPS: A: N45 33.578' / W116 50.041', 2,283 ft. (bridge in Imnaha); B: N45 42.069' / W116 50.041', 2,105 ft.

Best season: Summer

Land manager: Site A: Private—river access allowed. Site B: USFS—Wallowa-Whitman National Forest

Material: Porphyry basalt, agate, jasper

Tool: Geology pick

Vehicle: Any for Site A; 4WD for Site B

Accommodations: Imnaha River Inn Bed and Breakfast; camping on BLM land along Imnaha River

Special attraction: Hells Canyon

Finding the site: From Joseph, take OR 350 almost 30 miles to the town of Imnaha. Site A is found in "downtown" Imnaha at the bridge crossing the river. There are a few pullouts on the west side of the bridge. Find the trail leading down to the water. To get to Site B start up the hill in town and take a left onto Lower Imnaha Road. Drive 6.3 miles to where the pavement ends. Take the dirt road uphill. It will get pretty bumpy from here on in. Drive 7.4 miles down the steep curvy road until you find a good place to pull out and park. You will see the river to the east.

Rockhounding

The Imnaha River runs through some of the most beautiful scenery found in Oregon. Luckily a road runs right along with it most of the way and you can see it in its full glory. During low water levels search the gravels for agate, jasper, quartz, and porphyry basalt. The agate tends to be in the clear to blue tones with some banding. There is some nice yellow jasper along with bits of red and green. Hold out for good porphyry basalt with aesthetically pleasing shapes that look like chicken tracks or Asian writing.

Site A is located right smack in downtown Imnaha and can be accessed by any vehicle. Find the bridge, park, and then locate the trail that leads down to the river. For Site B you're going to need a much more rugged 4WD vehicle. The road is long and very bumpy, and I wouldn't ever want to be on it when it is wet. If you're back there and it starts to rain, you'd better hightail it out as quick and safely as possible.

South of town along Upper Imnaha Road are several more pullouts and the road is mostly gravel, but not that bad. I saw decent gravel deposits, but I couldn't really find a place to park during my visit. Every single spot was taken up by anglers. They were even camping in the road and I had to swerve around a tent. Another possible access point is at the Imnaha River Inn Bed and Breakfast. They allow anglers to access the river from the bridge by their property, but with permission only. It wouldn't hurt to stop in and ask at the inn. I hear they are very nice people.

About 15 miles up NF 4260 from Site B is a campground by the Snake River. I didn't make it up that far but I'm sure there are more access points to the Imnaha. The Snake River is also another good place to do some hunting. If you're up for an adventure, try your luck up there.

54. Murray Creek

An example of the abundant black marble found at Murray Creek.

See map on page 145.

Land type: Forested quarry

County: Wallowa

GPS: N45 22.403' / W117 21.260', 6,091 ft.

Best season: Summer

Land manager: Private—open by custom to casual collecting. Be on your best rockhounding behavior. If you come across "keep out" signs or fences, then respect the owners' rights and stay out.

Material: Marble, calcite, sea fossils

Tools: Geology pick, hammer, chisel, gad

Vehicle: 4WD suggested

Accommodations: Primitive camping allowed on BLM land; lodging in Enterprise

Special attractions: Town of Joseph; Wallowa Lake

Finding the site: From Enterprise, head east on OR 82 (Wallowa Lake Highway). You will be looking for Fish Hatchery Lane on the south side of the road about 1.5 miles out of town. Take Fish Hatchery Lane (which will turn into Powers Road) south for 0.9 mile. Take a right onto Reavis Lane and drive 1.2 miles to Lime Quarry Road. Take a left onto Lime Quarry and drive about 4 miles to the quarry. The road

The old quarry at Murray Creek has excellent black marble containing calcite crystals and fossils.

will get progressively worse from here on in. When you get near the quarry, a group of local dogs may come out to greet and escort you part of the way.

Rockhounding

Long ago this spot, near the town of Enterprise, was an active marble quarry. The mining activity has ceased and nowadays rockhounds, fossil collectors, and party animals are just about the only people who use this place. Rock carvers like this spot for its quality black marble, which makes striking sculptures. The size of the marble can be anywhere from tumbler size to massive boulders.

Marble found here is from the Hurwai Formation, which dates from the Triassic Period. Fossil sea life such as clams and brachiopods can be found within the black marble, as well as pockets of sparkly calcite. We found pockets of calcite formed in two crystal habits: dog-tooth, called so because it looks like a pointy canine tooth, and nail-head because, go figure, it looks like a nail.

Use caution while collecting close to the walls of the quarry. I wouldn't recommend climbing up the quarry, as the marble can be loose and may come tumbling down on unsuspecting rockhounds or slide out from under you. Although casual rockhounding is tolerated on this small chunk of private land, someone getting hurt would surely have it shut down quickly to collecting. Use common sense and be safe.

There is a very nice, yet small waterfall found in the quarry along with a weird, large stone platform. You'll see. Be on your best behavior while visiting, pack out any garbage, and try to leave it looking nicer than when you got there. There were many empty cases of cheap beer littered about when we visited. Rockhounds should always try their very hardest to stay in good standing with the public and leave few traces.

55. Lookout Point Reservoir

A collection of agate, jasper, and petrified wood found on the shore of Lookout Point Reservoir.

Land type: Reservoir shoreline
County: Lane
GPS: A: N43 50.519' / W122 37.066', 933 ft.; B: N43 50.516' / W122 37.543', 937 ft.
Best season: Summer–late fall
Land manager: USFS—Willamette National Forest
Material: Petrified wood, agate, jasper
Tool: Geology pick
Vehicle: Any
Accommodations: Primitive camping on site; campgrounds along Lookout Reservoir
Special attractions: The Office Bridge in Westfir (Oregon's longest covered bridge); McCreedy Hot Spring
Finding the site: From I-5 take exit 188 toward Oakridge and take OR 58 for about 23.2 miles. Keep your eyes peeled for a short little turnout on the right side of the road just past a nice turnout that is actually someone's driveway. This will be Site B. To reach Site A, continue east on OR 58 for 8.2 miles. Take a left onto Westfir Road. Drive about 0.4 mile across the bridge and continue to the left on Westfir Road for another 0.9 mile to Winfrey Road. Take a left across the bridge and continue along Winfrey for about 0.1 mile and take the fork to the right onto NF 5821 (N Shore Road). A couple miles in, the road will turn to small gravel. Drive 1.7 miles where you will cross some tracks and the road will fork. Continue to the left along NF 5821

Eugene to Canyonville

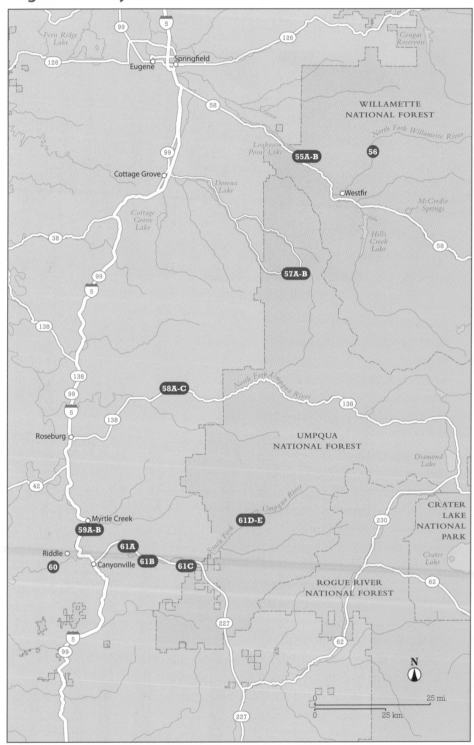

Low water levels are the best time for collecting at the shoreline of Lookout Point Reservoir.

for 2.8 miles where you will cross the tracks again. Take the road to the left onto W. Boundary Road and drive another 5 miles to the site, which will be on your left as you go around a corner. If you get to the fork of Boundary and NF 5824, you went just a bit too far. Site A can also be reached from Dexter via W. Boundary.

Rockhounding

At low water levels, during summer and fall, Lookout Point Reservoir is an excellent place to collect. The only drawback to this site is its accessibility. The two sites listed here are the only places I could find with a place to park and exposed gravels. If you are up for an adventure, drive all around the reservoir and maybe you will find a good spot. A boat would be the absolute best way to access otherwise unreachable spots. Luckily, there are plenty of boat launches to get started from.

Site A is found down a gravel road on the north side of the reservoir. There are a couple places to pull out and even a spot for primitive camping. Site B is somewhat sketchy. The pullout does not provide much room. There is a larger pullout just west of it, but it is a private driveway entrance. Once parked, you then have to run across the highway, cross some train tracks, and then scramble down a boulder-strewn hill to reach the shoreline. I definitely wouldn't visit this particular spot with children or pets. Site A would be much better with the little ones.

Once you have found your way to some good exposed gravel, put your head down and keep your eyes peeled. The most common material we found was low-grade petrified wood. It won't take much of a polish, but it has great cellular replacement and makes for some very pleasing specimen pieces. We found a fair amount of jasper during our visit. Most was red, but we found some small green pieces and one nice big red/yellow/orange chunk with some banded agate running through it. The agate was not as common, but what we found was good material. The most common variety we found was light blue and much of it had very tight banding. We also found a few tumble-worthy bits of multicolored agate. My score of the day was a bright orange piece of carnelian. It was small, but stunning.

56. North Fork Willamette River

Searching through the gravels of the North Fork for agates, jasper, and zeolites.

See map on page 152.

Land type: Gravel riverbank

County: Lane

GPS: N43 51.125' / W122 24.454', 1,407 ft.

Best season: Summer

Land manager: USFS—Willamette National Forest

Material: Zeolites, jasper, agate, petrified wood

Tools: Geology pick, hammer

Vehicle: Any

Accommodations: Camping throughout Willamette National Forest

Special attractions: The Office Bridge in Westfir (Oregon's longest covered bridge); McCreedy Hot Spring

Finding the site: From I-5 in Springfield, take exit 188 and head toward Oakridge on OR 58 (Willamette Highway). Drive about 31.3 miles to Westfir Road on your left. Take this road about 0.4 mile across the bridge where you will take a left and continue along N. Fork Road / Westfir Road through the town of Westfir. After

Westfir the road will turn into NF 19. Drive 11.1 miles to a bridge. About 0.1 mile past the bridge are a couple of turnouts that will get you close to the river.

Rockhounding

While this isn't a site I would recommend traveling long distances for, it's also not a complete waste of time. If you happen to be traveling or visiting the area, the North Fork of the Willamette River offers decent gravel bars to explore for common Oregon silicates. Agate, jasper, and zeolites are fairly plentiful along this beautiful scenic river.

This stretch of the Willamette is very popular with anglers, so during peak fishing season, finding a place to park can be somewhat tricky. The site mentioned here has a fair amount of parking space and is also close to a bridge where you can park. NF 19 runs along the North Fork Willamette River from Westfir to about Moolack Mountain. There are a lot of small pullouts along the way worth checking out for trails leading down to the river and gravel exposures. If you have time, be sure to explore.

After locating good gravel deposits, hike around and search them for material. Try to cover as much ground and gravel as possible. The agates we found were mostly small and clear to yellow toned. One piece had some nice banding. The jasper that decided to show itself was mostly red, yellow, or a combination of the two. We did find one very small piece of green jasper. The zeolites are found as blebs in basalt. Bring a good hammer to break open and expose any zeolite crystals hiding inside. We also were able to find one piece of low-grade petrified wood.

On your way to or from the site, be sure to stop and check out the Office Bridge in Westfir. It is the longest covered bridge in Oregon, at 180 feet. It is also the only covered bridge west of the Mississippi with a separate pedestrian walkway. The bridge is still in use and at one end is a park with picnic tables, trails, and restrooms.

57. Bohemia City

Tiny pyrite crystals found by smashing rocks at Site B in Bohemia City.

See map on page 152.

Land type: Forested mine dumps

County: Lane

GPS: A: N43 34.931' / W122 38.050', 4,345 ft. (Champion Mine); B: N43 34.772' / W122 39.196', 5,013 ft. (Bohemia City)

Best season: Summer

Land manager: Site A: USFS—Willamette National Forest; Site B: Private—open to collecting by custom. Be on your best behavior.

Material: Quartz, pyrite, chalcopyrite, bornite, galena, epidote, tourmaline

Tools: Geology pick, hammer, chisel

Vehicle: 4WD suggested

Accommodations: Campgrounds nearby; lodging and RV parks in Cottage Grove

Special attractions: Fairview Peak Lookout Tower; Bohemia Mining Days

Finding the site: From I-5 take exit 174 in Cottage Grove and head east on Row River Road. Continue along this road for about 18.5 miles and turn right onto Brice Creek Road. Travel about 8.3 miles to Champion Creek Road (NF 2259) and head up the hill. Drive about 5.2 miles to reach the Campion Mine (Site A). To reach Bohemia City continue along Champion Creek Road 0.4 mile where the road will

You can still see the old ore cart tracks leading out of the adit at the Musick Mine in Bohemia City.

turn right and into BLM 2560. Continue another 0.5 mile to a fork and take it to the right. Drive 0.4 mile to another fork. Take the fork to the left and drive about 0.5 mile until you reach Bohemia City.

Rockhounding

Bohemia City was once a bustling gold and silver mining region. Placer gold was discovered in Sharps Creek in 1858 and lode veins were soon after discovered by James Johnson. Johnson was from Bohemia in Europe, and thus the region was named after his homeland. Along with gold and silver come ores such as pyrite, chalcopyrite, bornite, and galena. Epidote crystals and low-grade schorl tourmaline are also found in these deposits.

Site A is the old Champion Mine. The area is under reclamation and is beginning to look much better than it did years ago. The old mine shaft is still there, but is locked up to keep the curious out. Search for material in the old tailing piles and throughout the hillsides. Bring a good hammer and be prepared to smash a lot of rocks open. Look for iron-stained rocks and purplish pieces of quartz. We found that iron ores were common inside these pieces of quartz. Many of the quartz chunks have small crystal pockets, and some can have pyrite or galena intermingling with the crystals. Tiny black tourmaline crystals can be found in matrix rock. Also look for nice green epidote.

Site B is the old Musick Mine located just above where Bohemia City was located. If you like old ghost towns, this is a fun place to visit. There are still cart tracks leading out of the mine to where they used to process the material. Most of the old buildings look as if the big bad wolf came along huffing and puffing, yet there is one rebuilt building still awkwardly standing. Look for the same material found at Site A as you search the tailing piles and the hills around the Musick Mine.

58. North Fork Umpqua River

Someone used this nice big piece of jasper as a stacking rock at the Umpqua River. I took it home.

See map on page 152.

Land type: Forested riverbank

County: Douglas

GPS: A: N43 19.351' / W123 03.419', 733 ft. (pullout); B: N43 19.558' / W123 00.993', 810 ft. (The Narrows); C: N43 19.997' / W123 00.291', 788 ft. (Swiftwater Recreation Site)

Best season: Summer

Land manager: BLM—Roseburg; USFS—Umpqua National Forest

Material: Jasper, agate, petrified wood

Tool: Geology pick for prying

Vehicle: Any

Accommodations: Camping in Umpqua National Forest; lodging in Glide, Roseburg, and Idleyld; RV parks in and near Idleyld Park and Roseburg

Special attractions: Rogue-Umpqua Scenic Byway; Umpqua Hot Springs; columnar basalt at Tokatee Falls

Finding the site: From I-5 exit 124 in Roseburg take OR 138 E/North Umpqua Highway east. Site A is about 20 miles from the exit. You will notice a small pullout on your right. Park here and locate the trail. Site B is another 2.1 miles east along OR 138. Again it will be found on your right. Park and locate a safe path to the river. Site C is another mile down the road and yes, it will be on your right. Park and find the gravel.

Search the gravels of the North Fork Umpqua River, even the human-piled rocks, for colorful agates and jaspers.

Rockhounding

The North Fork of the Umpqua River, one of Oregon's Scenic Waterways, offers a great opportunity for not only great rockhounding but great hikes offering vistas of beautiful waterfalls and access to a great hot springs. The agate found in the area is mostly clear to blue tones, but some excellent red carnelian can be obtained as well. The jasper can get fairly large and is found in red to yellow tones. Keep on the lookout for very rare teredo wood, a type of petrified wood with boreholes made in it before it was petrified.

Site A is a pullout that provides access to a great gravel bar to collect from and a bunch of excellent swimming holes. The only drawback is the trail leading down the hill to the riverbank is very steep. Be in good physical condition and wearing good footwear if attempting to scale the hillside. Look in the piles of rock that people stack up. I found a nice ten-pound chunk of jasper in one.

Site B is a picnic area called The Narrows. There is good gravel accumulation here, but as with Site A the hill leading to the riverbank is very steep. This is not a good spot for children or the elderly. For those in good physical condition, this is a chance to get on often unaccessed gravel bars, which means they are much less picked over. Site C is located at the Swiftwater Recreation Site and has easy access to gravel bars and a great plunge pool that is popular in the summer. Due to the easy access to this site, you're going to need to do some exploring in order to find areas that haven't been picked over. It is however the best spot to bring the kids and grandma.

There are lots of small pullouts along OR 138 with trails often used by fishermen. Test your luck and check out some of these spots. It helps to have a navigator sitting shotgun to help spot gravel bars while you drive the winding road. Try to time your visit for mid-summer, when the water level is low and before any river slime begins to develop and accumulate on the rocks.

59. Myrtle Creek

Typical red jasper, white quartz, and peachy sugar agate found in the gravels of the Umpqua River in Myrtle Creek.

See map on page 152.

Land type: River gravel bars

County: Douglas

GPS: A: N43 01.520' / W123 17.853', 603 ft. (parking area near freeway); B: N43 01.088' / W123 18.012', 589 ft. (access in town)

Best season: Summer

Land manager: BLM—Roseburg

Material: Quartz, chalcedony, agate, jasper, petrified wood

Tools: Geology pick, collecting bag

Vehicle: Most

Accommodations: Lodging and RV park in Myrtle Creek

Special attractions: Myrtle Creek–Canyonville Tour Route; Cow Creek Tour Route

Finding the site: From I-5 take the Myrtle Creek exit and head to Main Street and OR 99. Site A is just before the bridge heading into town. You will see a large parking area just above the river. Site B is found by heading into town. Drive about a mile in and take a right onto Western Avenue. At 0.1 mile you will cross railroad tracks. Stay to your left and take the dirt roads another 0.2 mile to the riverbank.

The trail leading down to Site A at Myrtle Creek. Cross the bridge and drive into town to reach Site B.

Rockhounding

The town of Myrtle Creek offers access near I-5 to the South Fork of the Umpqua River. There are many large gravel bars throughout the area. The GPS markings are sites where I found easy access to the river. More exploring of the area could prove to be a fruitful endeavor. Be respectful of private land. When I visited in the summer of 2012, they were building a new bridge across the river in the "middle" of town. This may be a good place to check for access when they are finished.

The material here is well worn and abundant. The gravel bars are huge. Quartz and chalcedony are the most abundant minerals. Keep a sharp eye tuned for elusive agates, some with quartz crystal pockets. Jasper is everywhere and can be found in tones of red, brown, and green; some is brecciated. I found many double-fist-size pieces, large enough to cut small slabs. Jasp-agate can be obtained as well.

By late summer many stretches of this river can get congested with colonies of algae and other river scum. They cover rock and make identifying minerals next to impossible. The cyanobacteria can also be harmful to humans and animals. They had warning signs posted on trees when I visited. Take care to wash your hands and your treasures to avoid any contamination.

60. Riddle

Look for green stains and coatings of garnierite on brown rocks at Riddle.

See map on page 152.
Land type: Mine tailings alongside road
County: Douglas
GPS: N42 55.738' / W123 24.833', 738 ft.
Best season: Any
Land manager: Private—Hanna Nickel Mine; open by custom to rockhounds
Material: Garnierite, chrysoprase
Tools: Hammer, chisel, gad
Vehicle: Any
Accommodations: None on site; RV park in Riddle
Special attractions: Cow Creek Tour Route; Myrtle Creek–Canyonville Tour Route
Finding the site: From I-5, take the Riddle exit, exit 103. Take OR 99, which will start off as Pruner Road and will turn into CR 39 (Glenbrook Loop Road) and then Cow Creek Road. From the exit travel 5.4 miles to Nickel Mine Road where you will take a right. A pullout next to a gate and a pile of rusty ore is to your immediate left. Park near the rocks on the outside of the gate. The site can also be reached from exits 98 and 101.

The nickel mine in Riddle leaves piles of rock near the entrance gate for rockhounds to dig through. Give them a wave as they drive in and out.

Rockhounding

The tailings pile from a shut down nickel mine provides the only opportunity in Oregon to find garnierite (a green nickel ore) and chrysoprase (chalcedony colored green by nickel). The top of Nickel Mountain was once a productive nickel mine from just after the Korean War up until about 1987. The nickel deposit is mostly depleted now and the new owners are using the slag for abrasive material. Luckily just a bit of the nickel still remains and the mine owners pile up potentially productive material for rockhounds to dig through near the entrance to the mine.

Use heavy hammers to break up material in hopes of exposing pockets of green. The garnierite is light to dark apple green and is found as coatings, veins, and masses in nickeliferous limonite. The chrysoprase is in the same color range but is extremely rare. I have seen some very small nice chunks come out of here, but you're going to have to be very lucky to find any. You most likely will not be walking out of this site with a tumbler load or anything worth cutting. Be happy with the specimens you're lucky enough to retrieve and leave plenty of rocks behind for the next rockhound.

For more information about Nickel Mountain, please consult *The Ore Bin*, Vol. 15, No. 10, October 1953.

61. South Fork Umpqua River

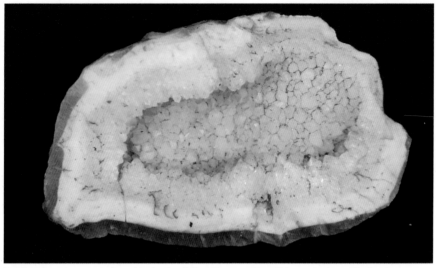

Here's a nice agate geode found in the South Fork Umpqua River. This one is about 5 inches long.

See map on page 152.

Land type: Forested riverbanks and creek banks

County: Douglas

GPS: A: N42 58.391' / W123 10.244', 778 ft. (bridge); B: N42 56.383' / W123 06.538', 848 ft. (dirt road); C: N42 55.937' / W122 59.485', 960 ft. (parking area); D: N43 02.187' / W122 48.608', 1,344 ft. (Dumont Campground); E: N42 01.972' / W122 46.315', 2,279 ft. (Zinc Creek)

Best season: Summer

Land manager: BLM—Roseburg; USFS—Umpqua National Forest

Material: Agate, jasper, quartz, schist, pyrite, carnelian

Tools: Geology pick, collecting bag

Vehicle: Any

Accommodations: Camping along South Fork Umpqua River

Special attractions: Myrtle Creek–Canyonville Tour Route; Cow Creek Tour Route

Finding the site: From I-5, take the Canyonville exit and travel east on OR 227. About 7 miles in you'll come to a bridge. This is Site A. The northeast side of the bridge has a narrow parking area and is where the trail leading to the riverbank

The bridge crossing the South Fork Umpqua River at Site A. There's a nice swimming hole here, so don't forget to bring a towel.

can be found. Site B is reached by traveling another 6.1 miles east on 227. There is a dirt road leading to the riverbank on your right (south). Take this road a couple hundred feet to a small parking area. You can see the gravel accumulations from here. Site C is reached by continuing east on 227 for about 9.5 miles to a rest area found on the right (south) side of the road just before reaching the town of Tiller. To reach Site D take Umpqua Road northeast from 227 going through Tiller. Take this road 3.6 miles to the Dumont campground found on your right (southeast). Park near the outhouse, where you will find a trail leading down to the riverbank. Zinc Creek (Site E) is reached by continuing northeast on Umpqua Road another 8.5 miles to NF 2980, which is a bridge on your right (south). Cross the bridge and travel 1.5 miles to a fork in the road. Take the road to the left and travel another 0.3 mile to a pullout on your left (north). Look for the trail leading to the plunge pool below the road.

Rockhounding

The following sites are all good spots to gain legal access to the South Fork Umpqua River. The only advantage to Sites C and E is that they have pit toilets. The method of attack at all the sites is the same; keep your head down, your eyes peeled, and inspect as much rock as you can. Wear shoes that are good for mucking around in shallow waters.

Tons of sugary white quartz cobbles can be found, along with some nice examples of sparkly schist. The river contains abundant agate. Most is clear, but can sometimes have a blue hue. Agates with quartz crystal centers can also be found. Rarely, carnelian may be obtained. You'll have better luck searching near where Zinc Creek enters the Umpqua. Jasper here tends to be red or brown; some may be brecciated. Low-grade petrified wood in mostly brown and gray tones can be found throughout the gravel bars as well.

Zinc Creek (Site E) is a great spot to find good, but very elusive deep red carnelian. Later in the summer season, fallen orange and red leaves can be distracting. Material can be found both up- and downstream from where the road crosses the creek. Search everywhere and move rocks around to find more material. Use the creek water to splash off dry accumulations of rock. Be on the lookout for low-grade petrified wood. The campground at the end of the bridge is a great place to camp primitively, if it's available.

Make sure to stop at the Bear Market in Tiller, especially if you need some supplies. While their inventory is limited, I always find myself stopping in for an ice-cream or firewood. They also have a small collection of stones that came out of the Umpqua River to check out at the counter. Stop in to get an idea what you're looking for. It's Tiller time!

62. Bullards Beach

A sample of the petrified wood, agate, and jasper commonly found at Bullards Beach.

Land type: Bay beach gravels
County: Coos
GPS: N43 08.614' / W124 24.605', 6 ft.
Best season: Winter–late spring
Land manager: Oregon Parks and Recreation Department: Bullards Beach State Park
Material: Jasper, petrified wood, agate, quartz
Tool: Geology pick
Vehicle: Any
Accommodations: Camping in state park; lodging in Bandon
Special attractions: Bandon Light House; Face Rock; Pacific Coast Scenic Byway
Finding the site: Bullards Beach is located north of Bandon off of US 101. Look for the signs leading to Bullards Beach State Park between mile markers 259 and 260. Drive 1.1 miles into the park till you find a small pullout on your left. Park here, follow the trail, and cross the creek to get to the gravel deposits.

South Coast

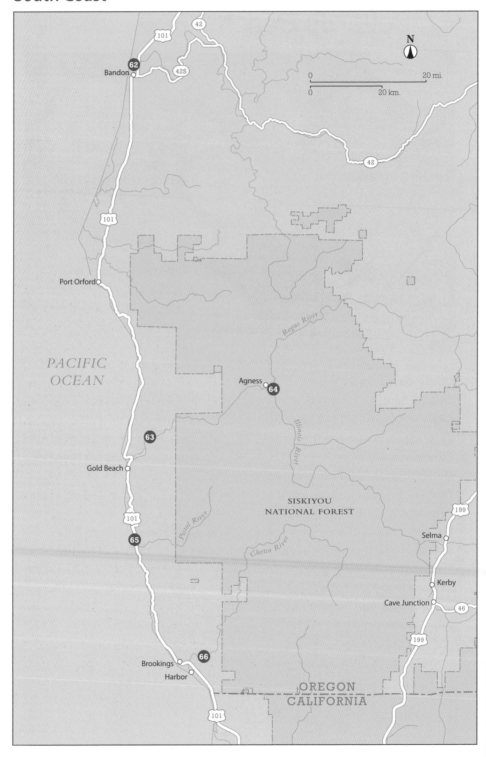

Search for abundant petrified wood in the gravels of the Coquille River at Bullards Beach State Park. Nasty rainy days like this one are great for beach hunting.

Rockhounding

A very productive gravel deposit can be found on the bay side of Bullards Beach State Park. The ocean side of the park is usually covered by sand, but always worth checking for gravels. In Oregon the beaches are public land up to the high water mark. The nearby lighthouse is well worth a visit while in the park. If you're an equestrian, the state park also provides horse camping and access to good trails.

This beach is well known for its abundance of good-quality petrified wood. I have never found so much petrified wood on a beach before. The wood tends to be in gray and brown tones, but there are some pieces with some red in them. It is highly silicified and takes a great polish when tumbled. Larger pieces could yield some small slabs. I found one that was about 5 by 5 inches, exhibiting great growth rings.

There is also plentiful jasper found in an array of colors. It can be red, yellow, green, brown or a combination of two or more colors. Even the red jasper is bright and is often brecciated with white quartz. If you're tired of plain old red beach jasper, this beach offers something a bit more exciting.

The agate on this beach tends to be a bit sugary, but the variety of color keeps it interesting. With some diligent searching some nice clear agates can be found too. Sally and I found some nice fancy agates and some with banding. You will find loads of sugary white quartz and other interesting breccias and colorful stones here as well.

There are many other places nearby to find potentially productive beaches. These stops include Bandon State Park, Whiskey Run, Seven Devils Wayside, and Cape Arago. If one beach isn't producing, move on to the next.

63. Rogue River—Orchard Bar

Lots of good red brecciated jasper can be found in the Rouge River.

See map on page 168.

Land type: Riverbank gravels

County: Curry

GPS: N42 27.876' / W124 22.109', 20 ft.

Best season: Winter

Land manager: BLM—Coos

Material: Quartz, agate, jasper, petrified wood

Tool: Geology pick

Vehicle: 4WD suggested

Accommodations: Primitive camping allowed on site; lodging in Gold Beach; camping and RV parks along US 101

Special attractions: Sixes River Recreation Site; Pacific Coast Scenic Highway

Finding the site: From US 101 (Pacific Coast Scenic Highway) in Gold Beach, take CR 595 east along the Rogue River. It will eventually turn into Jerry's Flat Road. At about 4 miles from the highway, you will notice some gravel roads on your left heading to the river. Pick one your vehicle can handle and drive to the river and park. It's a good idea to have 4WD if you plan on driving on the gravel or if it's wet. If you have a low-clearance vehicle, park near the road and hike the short distance in. There are even more pullouts with access to the river farther along Jerry's Flat Road.

Parked on the huge gravel deposit at Orchard Bar.

Rockhounding

The gravel bar at this spot on the Rouge River is absolutely huge. It's also very popular with anglers and river tours. During the summer tourist season, you will see many jetboats cruising up and down the river and it can be quite loud at times. I have visited this site during winter and found much of the gravel exposed, yet there were absolutely no loud boats and it rained just enough to make the good silicate material stand out. It may have been a bit cold and wet, but if you're a true Oregon rockhound you're used to it and know the rain actually benefits in identification.

Look for your usual Oregon river rocks: quartz, jasper, and agate. The white quartz is the most abundant, followed by red brecciated jasper. Most of the jasper is a brick-red tone, but some bright-red, brown, and green pieces can be found. The agate is mostly clear, but with some luck you'll find some with banding and possibly some carnelian. Most of the material that has made it this far down the river has been very well tumbled and rounded. Keep your eyes peeled for small amounts of brown petrified wood. Wet weather helps to identify rocks that will take a good polish.

Camping on site is generally allowed, but there are no facilities or designated spaces, so keep that in mind. Keep an eye out for signs in case things change. If you camp, leave the site cleaner than when you found it. We want rockhounds to have and keep a good reputation with the local communities.

64. Rogue River—Agness

This colorful agate was trying to hide from me until I was almost about to leave. I found it right next to my truck as it started to rain.

See map on page 168.

Land type: Riverbank gravels

County: Curry

GPS: N42 33.080' / W124 04.004', 141 ft.

Best season: Low water levels

Land manager: USFS—Rouge River / Siskiyou National Forest

Material: Quartz, jasper, agate, petrified wood, gold

Tool: Geology pick

Vehicle: 4WD suggested

Accommodations: Lodging in Gold Beach; camping and RV parks along Rouge River

Special attraction: Pacific Coast Scenic Highway

Finding the site: This is a long and curvy drive. Be prepared for rock slides as well. From US 101 (Pacific Coast Scenic Highway) in Gold Beach take CR 595 east along the Rogue River. It will eventually turn into Jerry's Flat Road. From the highway travel approximately 32 miles, then turn left onto CR 375 and follow the signs to Agness. Drive down CR 375 for about 3 miles past the store in Agness and down the hill. The last 0.2 mile or so is gravel and dirt and the end is very steep. 4WD is suggested for this last stretch, especially if it is wet.

Agness: where the Illinois River meets the Rouge River. Search the gravels for good agate and jasper.

Rockhounding

The historic town of Agness is located at the junction of the Rouge and Illinois Rivers. The gravel bar located here is usually larger in the summer during low water levels, but I have had decent luck at this site even in January. This spot, like many on the Rouge River, is a very popular location with anglers, and parking can be limited at times. You may have to park up the road and hike in if it's crowded at the river, or if you don't have faith in your vehicle making it down and back up the steep hill.

You're going to find lots of white quartz and red jasper, just like at many Oregon riverbank gravels. Much of the jasper is brecciated and can also be found in tones of brown and green. I have found a few large agates at this spot over the years; some were carnelian and many were banded. Most of the agate found is going to be clear to gray/blue tones. Gold panners can try their luck finding paydirt here. The Rouge River has long been known for its gold deposits and there are still claims in the area. Being that the Illinois River dumps out into the Rouge here, there is a slim possibility of finding the rare mineral josephinite—slim, but not impossible.

Be sure to bring some good mucking shoes for exploring the shallow areas, but use caution and don't wade out too far into the river. The Rouge has a very strong current and frequently passing jetboat tours create quite a wake that can sweep you off your feet. As with all gravel deposit rockhounding, rain can be your friend. Good hard silicate material stands out against the other rocks when it is wet and the dirt is washed off.

65. Pistol River

A bright piece of red jasper trying to hide under plant debris at the Pistol River.

See map on page 168.

Land type: Riverbank gravels

County: Curry

GPS: N42 16.639' / W124 24.191', 2 ft.

Best season: Any

Land manager: BLM—Coos Bay

Material: Quartz, jasper, agate, petrified wood

Tool: Geology pick

Vehicle: Any

Accommodations: Lodging in Gold Beach and Brookings; camping and RV parking along US 101

Special attraction: Pacific Coast Scenic Highway

Finding the site: The Pistol River is easily reached from US 101 (Pacific Coast Scenic Highway). Look for the Pistol River State Scenic Wayside about halfway between Gold Beach and Brookings. The wayside is on the southwest side of the bridge that crosses the Pistol River. Park in the lot and hike your way under the bridge to the main gravel deposits.

US 101 crossing the Pistol River. Parking is near the southwest side of the bridge. Take your eyes off the rocks every now and then to look for otters in the river.

Rockhounding

This site is easily reached from the highway and makes a good spot for those without a lot of time traveling along US 101, as a good gravel bar is just a brief hike from the parking area near the bridge. I often see otters in this river and they always seem to distract me from keeping my eyes on the rocks. Being so near the ocean, this river site is affected by tides; the river's depth will change with little notice and seem to flow back upstream. Wear shoes you don't mind getting wet.

Abundant white quartz and red brecciated jasper can be found in the gravels. The jasper seems to be a bit brighter than the common brick-red variety found throughout Oregon. It can also be found in tones of brown and green. The agate is mostly clear with some banding. Carnelian and other colors are less common, but can be obtained. Small amounts of petrified wood can be found, but it's pretty rare. The good news is if it made it this far down the river, then it is most likely hard and will take a good polish. There are reports of jade found in this river, but I have never found nor seen any of it.

For even more rockhound adventuring, find your way across the river via Frontage Road about a half mile south of the wayside. Work your way up into the national forest land and look for more gravel deposits that are going to be much less picked over. Steer clear of private land on your way in. The presence of fences and signs are great ways to tell if land is private or not.

66. Chetco River

Big red brecciated jasper found in the shallows of the Chetco River.

See map on page 168.
Land type: Riverbank
County: Curry
GPS: N42 03.841' / W124 13.779', 19 ft.
Best season: Any
Land manager: BLM—Coos Bay
Material: Quartz, jasper, agate
Tool: Geology pick
Vehicle: Any
Accommodations: Lodging in Brookings and Harbor; camping and RV parks along US 101 and the Chetco River
Special attraction: Pacific Coast Scenic Byway
Finding the site: From US 101 (Pacific Coast Scenic Byway) in Brookings at Azalea State Park, take CR 787, which will turn into North Bank Chetco River Road. Travel 3.4 miles from the highway and look for a turnout/parking area to your right. There should be a sign saying "Social Security Bar" on it. If your vehicle can't make it to the gravel itself, then park here and hike the short distance in. If you can make it to the gravel, find a place to park and begin exploring.

The huge gravel deposit at Social Security Bar on the Chetco River. Attendance was light on this day. There are usually many more trucks.

Rockhounding

The Chetco River is host to some absolutely huge gravel bars. Social Security Bar—so named because of the number of retirees who fish here—could keep any rockhound busy for hours. It is also very close to the highway, making for a good spot to visit while traveling. Some of the anglers will give you an odd look as you walk back and forth searching the gravels. Areas like this are why I leave my fishing pole and license at home. A good fishing hole can be very distracting for me when rockhounding.

If red brecciated jasper is your thing, this is the site for you. Large double-fist-size pieces and larger can be easily acquired during your hunt. Brown jasper can be found as well. Like in most southwestern Oregon rivers, there are loads of white quartz all over. I found that the quartz found in the Chetco is a little bit more translucent than most. I also found a few pieces with small druzy quartz pockets. For white quartz it was fairly interesting. Watch for agate and carnelian. I did not find a lot during my visit, but that doesn't mean it's not there. I have seen some decent agates come from this spot. There is also always potential for petrified wood.

67. Josephine Creek

A small pile of josephinite, courtesy of Hampton's Rock Shop in Kerby. Specimens average around ¼ inch.

Land type: Forested creek bank
County: Josephine
GPS: N42 14.513' / W123 41.088', 1,199 ft.
Best season: Summer
Land manager: USFS—Rouge River / Siskiyou National Forest
Material: Serpentine, josephinite
Tools: Gold pan, metal detector
Vehicle: 4WD suggested
Accommodations: Campground on site; Illinois River State Park
Special attraction: Oregon Caves
Finding the site: From I-5 take US 199 (Redwood Highway) from Grants Pass toward Cave Junction. Just south of Selma take a right onto 8 Dollar Mountain Road. Drive about 2.9 miles to an outhouse and take a left over the bridge. From the bridge, drive up the hill 0.4 mile to a campground. Park at the Josephine Creek campground and hike to the creek from here.

Rockhounding

Josephine Creek is known for two rare and unusual nickel–iron minerals called josephinite and oregonite. These minerals were designated the official

Southwest

The site at Josephine Creek. We only found serpentine, but had a great time trying.

Oregon State twin-minerals in 2013. They resemble nickel-iron meteorites and were once believed to be extraterrestrial, though science has proved that the material is of earthly origin. Both minerals feature unusual geometric patterns in their matrices known as Widmanstatten patterns, which are also found in meteorites. Much is still unknown about these minerals; scientists theorize that the material came from deep within the Earth's lower mantle, but the minerals' origin has yet to be confirmed. Josephinite is metallic gray; oregonite is brown. Josephinite is also magnetic, whereas oregonite is not, making this an easy way to distinguish between the two.

The first thing you're going to need in order to find josephinite is a lot of luck. Diligent searching is a close second. Watch for small rounded metal nuggets resembling tarnished silver. You can walk around and test your luck at surface collecting, or you can stick a pan in the creek and see what turns up. Black sands are common in this area and may contain metals such as gold and platinum. Save your sands for more fun back at home. A metal detector would be a very handy tool for this kind of hunting. Plan your trip for low water for better gravel exposure.

To get an idea of what you're looking for, make a stop at either the Hampton's Rock Shop in nearby Kerby or The Crystal Kaleidoscope in Selma. They both have wonderful shops with lots of local minerals and usually have some josephinite and serpentine on hand to check out.

What *is* commonly found in the area is lots and lots of serpentine. The local hills are made out of it. Check the hills and creek for sizeable and high-quality solid specimens. The color runs from light to dark green and black.

68. Althouse Creek

A large slab of pink rhodonite from Althouse Creek. Rice Northwest Museum of Rocks and Minerals specimen

See map on page 179.

Land type: Forest riverbank
County: Josephine
GPS: N42 06.343' / W123 31.434', 1,737 ft.
Best season: Late spring—early fall
Land manager: BLM—Medford
Material: Serpentine, rhodonite
Tools: Geology pick, hammer
Vehicle: Any
Accommodations: Campgrounds along OR 46; lodging in Cave Junction
Special attractions: The Oregon Caves National Monument; Crystal Kaleidoscope (Selma); Hampton's Rock Shop (Kerby)
Finding the site: From US 199 (Redwood Highway) through Cave Junction, take OR 46 east toward the Oregon Caves National Monument. Drive 1.8 miles to Holland Loop Road on your right. Take Holland Loop 5.3 miles and take a right onto Althouse Creek Road. Drive approximately 2.3 miles until you start seeing spur roads on your right that will take you down to the river. Pick a road, find the river, and start hunting.

Sally inspecting suspect material for traces of pink rhodonite. Don't forget your hammer; you'll need it at this site.

Rockhounding

Southwestern Oregon is a good location to find the pink manganese oxide known as rhodonite, but it's not easy. From what locals and rock shop owners tell me, Althouse Creek is about the only easily accessible spot in the area where one might find the elusive pink lapidary material. The Rouge Gem and Geology Club also holds a rhodonite claim in the area. You may want to try hooking up with them for some fun hard-rock mining.

There are many pullouts and spur roads that will take you down to the creek from Althouse Creek Road. Once you get into BLM land, start looking for them. My GPS was just one of many spots you will find up to about milepost 5. Park your vehicle and make your way down to the creek. Search the gravels for pink. Manganese oxidizes black, so you may have to split suspect material open to find the pink. Bring a good heavy hammer and get to swinging.

Don't hold your breath on finding rhodonite. I've been to this spot twice now and haven't found anything but chips. It gives me hope though, and the good material is really nice. If you really need a piece of southwestern Oregon rhodonite and you can't find any yourself, pay a visit to one of the local rock shops for some. Hampton's Rock Shop in nearby Kerby has some excellent material for sale.

One thing there is plenty of in the area is excellent serpentine. Search for it in the creek gravels or look for outcrops. It's not hard to find. The serpentine is somewhat waxy, with color ranging dark to light green with some black. It makes excellent carving material, although it does contain asbestos. Use caution and be smart when working with this beautiful mineral.

69. Powell Creek

A small chunk of soapstone found at Powell Creek. Note the scratch test mark on the bottom right corner.

See map on page 179.

Land type: Forested road cut

County: Josephine

GPS: N42 15.609' / W123 19.093', 2,450 ft.

Best season: Late spring–fall

Land manager: BLM—Medford

Material: Soapstone

Tools: Geology pick, hammer, chisel, gad, pocket knife

Vehicle: 4WD

Accommodations: Camping allowed on BLM land

Special attractions: Historic Jacksonville; Crystal Kaleidoscope (Selma); Hampton's Rock Shop (Kerby)

Finding the site: If coming from Grants Pass, take OR 238 (Williams Highway) toward Jacksonville for approximately 6.7 miles. Take a right onto Water Gap Road and drive 2.7 miles to Upper Powell Creek Road where you will take a right. Drive 3.2 miles and take a left onto BLM 38-5-17.1 and drive about 0.8 mile to the road cut at the curve. There will be a decent place to pull out on your left. This site can also be reached from the west through Selma by taking Deer Creek Road / Cedar Flat Road east until you meet up with Water Gap Road.

Inspecting the talus of the road cut at Powell Creek.

Rockhounding

The area found between Grants Pass and south of Cave Junction into California is well known by rockhounds and rock carvers for its abundant soapstone deposits. The only drawback is finding good accessible exposures. The terrain in this part of Oregon is steep and rugged to say the least. Locals who know the area well do a lot of hiking for their choice pieces of soapstone. Powell Creek doesn't offer the *highest* quality soapstone in the world. It's a bit hard for high-quality material, but the good news is that it is a pretty green, suited for carving, and most importantly it is accessible. There is a nice road cut exposure at this site.

Find your way to the road cut and park. The soapstone here is generally in the dark green tones. You will find plenty of small- to medium-size pieces that have weathered out of the exposure and rolled down the hill. Most soapstone should be soft enough to scratch with your fingernail. As I mentioned, this material is a bit harder than most. Bring a pocket knife or a steel nail to scratch test any suspect material.

For larger chunks you'll have to work it out of the road cut. If you happen to knock any debris into the road while doing this, please be courteous and pick up any rubble. I know that the road in is fairly nasty and there are rocks everywhere, but I would hate to see a place get shut down due to a few lazy rockhounds. Do some exploring of the area and maybe you'll get lucky and find another good soapstone exposure.

70. Agate Desert

A sample of tumbler-worthy agate, jasper, and petrified wood found in the sticky mud at Denman Wildlife Area.

See map on page 179.

Land type: Open fields; lakeshore

County: Jackson

GPS: A: N42 25.027' / W122 52.271', 1,280 ft. (Denman Wildlife Area); B: N42 24.651' / W122 46.228', 1,512 ft. (Agate Lake)

Best season: Summer

Land manager: Jackson County—Agate Lake Recreation Area; ODFW—Ken Denman Wildlife Area

Material: Agate, petrified wood

Tool: Geology pick

Vehicle: Any

Accommodations: None on site; hotels, motels, and RV parks in area

Special attraction: Lake of the Woods Highway

Finding the site: Denman Wildlife Area (Site A) can be reached from I-5 by taking exit 30. Head east on OR 62 (Crater Lake Highway) and drive for 4.9 miles. Take a right onto Agate Road and drive 0.1 mile, then take a left onto Gregory Road and travel another 0.5 mile to a sharp left turn. Continue straight and pay the fee at the office. Site A is found by walking down the trail. It's paved at first, and then turns to dirt as it passes around willows that shade fishing holes and sleeping ducks, with the pond to your right. Continue past the pond until you get to a fence. The scraped areas beyond here are where you want to search.

To reach the western shore of Agate Lake, from I-5 in Medford take exit 30. Take OR 62 (Crater Lake Highway) east about 5.5 miles to OR 140 E (Lake of the Woods Highway). Take OR 140 3.6 miles, then take a right onto Antelope Road. Follow Antelope for 0.7 mile and take a very sharp right onto Agate Dam Access Road. Follow the road 0.8 mile to the parking lot.

To reach the eastern shore of Agate Lake, from I-5 in Medford take exit 30. Take OR 62 (Crater Lake Highway) east about 5.5 miles to OR 140 E (Lake of the Woods Highway). Take OR 140 3.6 miles, then take a right onto Antelope Road. Drive 1.9 miles, staying to your right till you get to Dry Creek Road. Take a right and drive 0.6 mile to the county park where you will easily find the lakeshore.

Rockhounding

Ken Denman Wildlife Area and Agate Lake lie within the once very productive area known as the Agate Desert. Over the years the city has grown and much of the land is either built on or is now private property. The wildlife area and the lake are now just about the only places to gain legal access. There is agate, jasper, and petrified wood found just about everywhere around this

A little rain can't prevent true rockhounds from collecting at Agate Lake.

area. It's called the Agate Desert for good reason. If you know people in the area, or are willing to hunt down land owners, you may be able to gain access to some very worthwhile spots.

To collect at the Ken Denman Wildlife Area, you must first obtain a collecting permit along with a parking permit from the offices found on site. The collecting permit is free, but there is a nominal parking fee. You'll find lots of great tumbler-size material at the wildlife area. The agate is plentiful and is mostly in tones of gray, blue, and red. Some is banded, botryoidal, and/or contains some small pockets of small quartz crystals. The jasper is found in bright tones of red, yellow, brown, and/or green. Much of the jasper is very hard and will take an excellent polish in a tumbler. The petrified wood is generally found in natural wood tones and has good cellular replacement. If you visit the area during wet weather, be sure to wear some good mucking shoes. The mud here is super sticky and is like concrete when it dries.

Visit Agate Lake during low water levels, as more gravel will be exposed and you'll have a better chance of finding larger tumbler material. Wear shoes you don't mind getting dirty, and that will also stay securely on your feet in case of sticky, deep mud. Don't expect to walk away with a full bucket as material is sparse and generally small at this location. The agate is mostly clear, but some can have a slight blue tint or banding. The petrified wood is mostly in the brown tones, but some reddish material can be found as well.

71. Emigrant Lake

A view to the east over Emigrant Lake from Site B.

See map on page 179.
Land type: Lakeshore gravel beds
County: Jackson
GPS: A: N42 09.509' / W122 37.007', 2,240 ft. (boat launch); B: N42 08.471' / W122 37.233', 2,235 ft. (dirt road pullout)
Best season: Summer
Land manager: Jackson County—Emigrant Lake Recreation Area
Material: Agate, jasper
Tool: Collecting bag
Vehicle: Any
Accommodations: Developed camping on site; lodging in Ashland
Special attractions: ScienceWorks Hands On Museum; Oregon Shakespeare Festival
Finding the site: From I-5 in Ashland (exit 14) take OR 66 (Green Springs Highway) east. Travel 3.3 miles to the turn on your left for Emigrant Lake County Park. It's less than a mile to the fee booth. From here find an open parking area with easy access to the lake. I made my GPS marking near the boat launch. For the free experience continue past the turn for the state park and keep an eye out for dirt roads on

your left. There will be three or four for the next couple miles with access to the lake. The first dirt road is where I made my GPS marking for Site B.

Rockhounding

Large and well-rounded agate and jasper are abundant in the gravels of Emigrant Lake. The problem is the gravels themselves are not as abundant. Be sure to time your trip late in the summer season to ensure good gravel exposure. I found that the quality and amount of material was better in the state park, though there is a modest fee to use the park. Picnic tables, boat ramps, and a playground are available. Camping and RV hookups are also provided at the park for another nominal fee. There's even a 280-foot twin flume waterslide! I can't think of any other rockhounding sites with a waterslide available.

Be sure to visit the lake during low water levels as there will be much more gravel exposed. Once you find good gravel exposures, collecting material is very easy. You just walk around and pick it up. You'll see lots of sugary white quartz scattered about everywhere. The agate tends to be sugary too. It won't take much of a polish, but pieces tend to be large and colorful and would look great in a water feature. The jasper is mostly brown, green, or a combination of the two.

Farther east on OR 66 are many rock outcrops along the road. Reports say that the host rock can contain agate, quartz, and common opal. I found a nice pullout near milepost 13 that gets you well off the road. Though I never had much luck at this pullout, I've heard reports of nice pieces being found, so I figured I would mention the spot.

72. Rabbit Basin

An Oregon sunstone sunset. Sunstone pulled off the Spectrum Mine belt.

Land type: High desert sagebrush
County: Lake
GPS: A: N42 43.391' / W119 51.645', 4,625 ft. (public area sign); B: N42 43.993' / W119 52.075', 4,644 ft. (Spectrum Mine); C: N42 42.863' / W119 51.972', 4,605 ft. (Dust Devil Mine); D: N42 42.758' / W119 49.248', 4,627 ft. (Double Eagle Mine)
Best season: Summer
Land manager: BLM—Lakeview; private (mines)
Material: Sunstones
Tools: Geology pick, pick, hammer, chisel, shovel, screen
Vehicle: Any
Accommodations: Primitive camping on site; lodging in Plush
Special attractions: Hart Mountain Hot Springs; Hart Mountain Antelope Refuge; Oregon Outback Scenic Byway
Finding the site: From US 20 in Riley, travel 65.7 miles south on US 395. Turn left (east) onto Country Road 3-10 (Hogback Road). The roads will be gravel from here on in. Travel 20.2 miles and take a left onto Country Road 3-11. Head 0.5 mile and turn left onto BLM Road 6155. Follow 6155 for about 8.2 miles. Take a left onto BLM Road 6115. The turn for the public area (Site A) is located about 5 miles in.

Sunstones

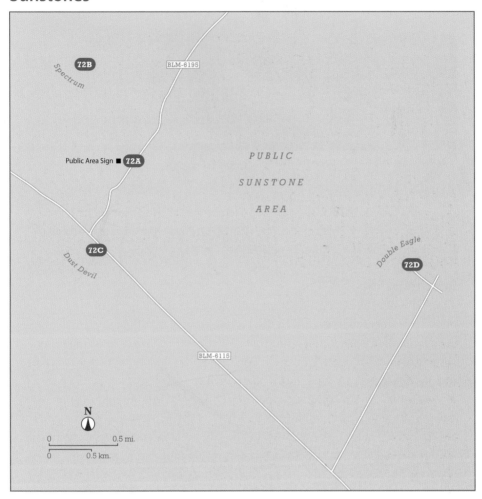

Along the way you will pass Double Eagle and Dust Devil mines. Look for the Double Eagle sign on your right (Site D). The mine is another 1.8 miles down the dirt road. Dust Devil (Site C) is another 1.2 miles along 6115 from the Double Eagle entrance and is easily seen from the road. To reach the public area, drive 0.1 mile past Dust Devil and take a right (northeast) onto BLM Road 6195 and continue 0.6 mile until you see the sign. The Spectrum Mine (Site B) is located within the public collecting area and is reached by taking the third left off of 6195. There should be a small sign pointing the way.

The processing belt at Spectrum Sunstone Mine.

From Plush take Country Road 3-10 (Hogback Road) north for about 10 miles where you will turn right onto Country Road 3-11. Follow previous instructions from here. Hogback will turn to gravel about 4 miles in.

Rockhounding

The Lakeview District BLM has kindly set aside 2,500 acres of land in the high desert for rockhounds to collect a unique variety of plagioclase feldspar found only in Oregon, called sunstone. What makes Oregon sunstone unique is the presence of copper in the crystals. This simple element creates colors such as red, green, or blue and a phenomenon called schiller. Schiller refers to stones that have a layer of copper that "blinks" at you. Oregon named the sunstone its official state gemstone in 1987.

Primitive camping is allowed in the public area and there is room for RVs to park. There are a couple of picnic tables and shade structures, and a pit toilet available for public use. Other than that, you're on your own. This is a very remote area. Make sure to bring in plenty of supplies, as the nearest convenience store and gas station is 43 miles away in Plush. I must say they make a great burger in Plush. Lakeview offers more amenities, but is 56 miles from the digging area.

Sunstones found in the public area are mostly clear yellow, with the occasional schiller. The material tumbles excellently, so be sure to pick up enough to charge a load. This is easily accomplished, because there is sunstone everywhere. All you need to do is walk around and pick them up. Even the ants use tiny jewel fragments on their hills. Wander away from the beaten path for better chances of finding larger stones. Watch for claim boundaries and don't collect on claims unless invited to do so by the claim holders. Keep the sun in front of you, as it illuminates the stones. It also helps to collect just after a rare, light rain shower. The freshly washed stones glow like homing beacons for crystal hunters. If you have a screen, try your luck at finding larger stones by digging some holes. Remember to fill in your holes when you're done.

To find rare and prized colored stones, you will need to go to a fee mine. The mine owners are all very friendly and welcome rockhounds of all experience levels. At the time of publication, three fee mine operations were available to the public. Spectrum, Dust Devil, and Double Eagle provide an opportunity to find prized colored sunstones. Each mine has a different mode of attack, ranging from digging and screening in pits and from condensed ore piles to picking stones *I Love Lucy* style off of processing belts. Prices vary at each mine as well. Information is very easy to find online; please contact the mines to inquire about pricing and availability. The mines are generally open May–October, weather permitting. Mines provide free camping and pit toilets on site for those digging at their mine. The Spectrum Mine also offers a tee-pee, simple cabins, and hot showers free for paying prospectors. The teepee is my personal favorite place to stay when visiting the area. Call or e-mail ahead for reservations.

Sunstones in a gold pan. I get more use out of my gold pan this way.

73. Flook Lake

Search for dark jasper and colorful agates throughout the dry lakebed of Flook Lake.

Land type: High desert dry lakebed
County: Lake
GPS: N42 34.529' / W119 31.841', 5,079 ft.
Best season: Late spring–fall
Land manager: BLM—Lakeview
Material: Agate, jasper
Tool: Collecting bag
Vehicle: Any
Accommodations: Camping in designated areas in Hart Mountain National Antelope Refuge; lodging in Plush
Special attractions: Hart Mountain National Antelope Refuge; Hart Mountain Hot Springs; Oregon Outback Scenic Byway
Finding the site: From Hogback Road in Plush, take Hart Mountain Road. Follow this road all the way up the mountain for about 23 miles until you get to the refuge headquarters. From the headquarters take the fork in the road to the east heading toward Frenchglen. This is Frenchglen Road. Travel 6.7 miles to a dirt road on your right. This is Flook Lake Road. Head down this road about 1.5 miles to the GPS reading that I took by the mounds in the middle of the lakebed. The collecting area begins about where the sagebrush ends. Look for gravel deposits.

South Central

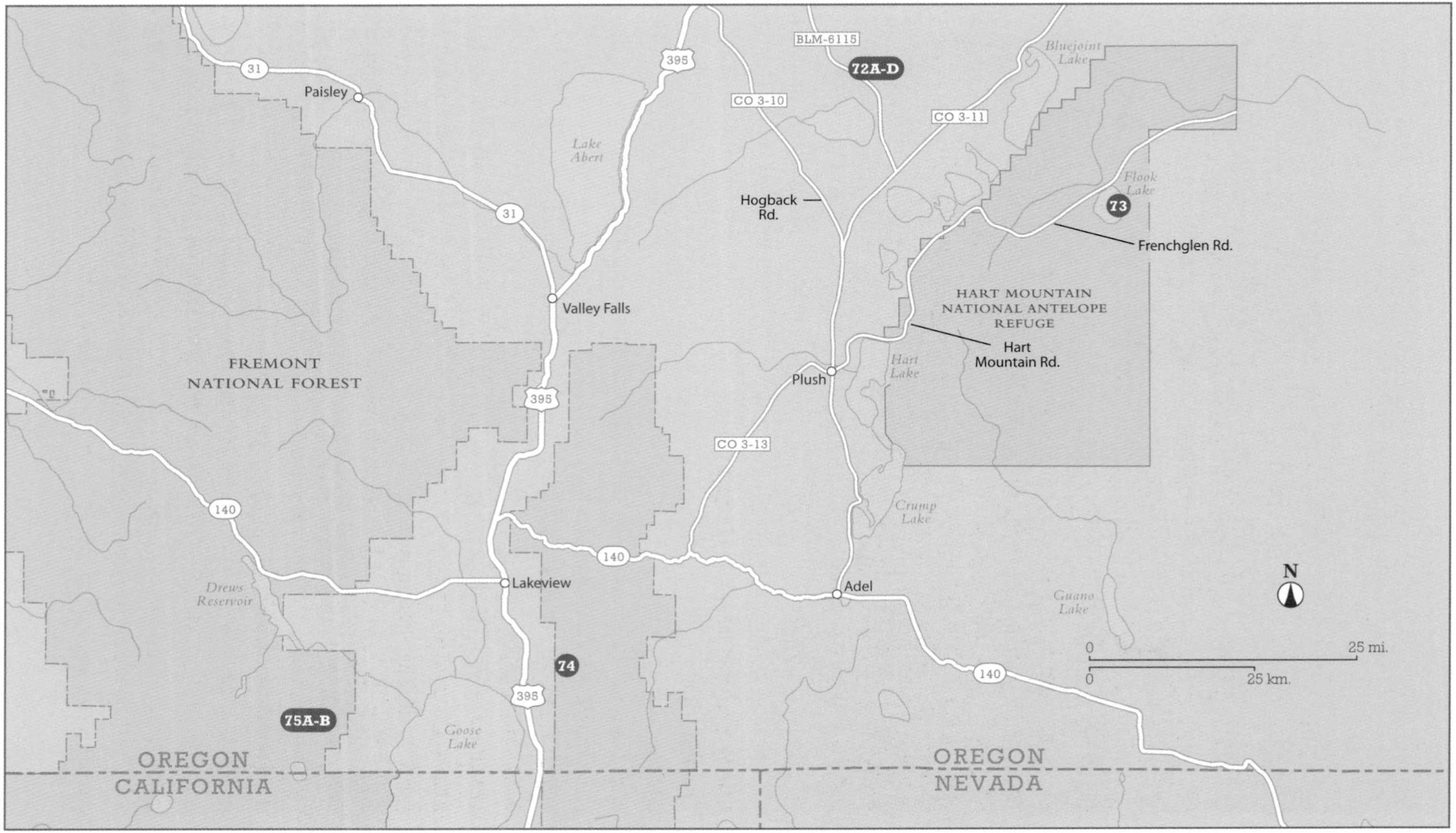

Frenchglen Rd.

73

Bluejoint Lake

Flook Lake

HART MOUNTAIN
NATIONAL ANTELOPE
REFUGE

Hart
Mountain Rd.

CO 3-11

BLM-6116

72A-D

Hart Lake

Crump Lake

Guano Lake

CO 3-10

Hogback
Rd.

Plush

CO 3-13

Adel

140

OREGON
NEVADA

395

Lake
Abert

Valley Falls

395

140

Lakeview

74

395

Goose
Lake

31

Paisley

FREMONT
NATIONAL FOREST

140

Drews
Reservoir

75A-B

OREGON
CALIFORNIA

N

25 mi.

25 km.

Taking an easy stroll on dry Flook Lake. Head toward the dark spots that often contain agate and jasper.

Rockhounding

Flook Lake is a dry lakebed located atop the Hart Mountain National Antelope Refuge. This location makes for a nice day getaway if you're spending some time mining at the nearby sunstone mines. Not only is the material very nice and plentiful, but there is a great hot springs located just a few miles away. I always take an opportunity to take a soak there while in the area. There are excellent vistas of the surrounding valleys, lakes, and hills. Keep an eye out for herds of antelope throughout the refuge and bighorn sheep in the hillsides.

Agate and jasper are the main minerals found at Flook Lake. The agates and jaspers have been weathered to an almost fine polish. Look for dark patches throughout the lakebed. These are deposits of rocks and contain what you're looking for here. The agate I found was mostly in brown and yellow tones to almost carnelian tones. I guess a lot of the agate could be classified as sard. There are references in literature to there being a blue-toned agate here, but I didn't see any myself. The agate tends to be small, but is very good for tumbling. The jasper is mostly tan to dark brown, but can also be found in tones of red and even green. It can range from tumbler-size material to rarer fist-size pieces. Because this is a wildlife refuge, you are limited to surface collecting only, no digging. You are also restricted to seven pounds of material per person, per day.

During fire season many of the side roads including the one leading to this site can be closed. Be sure to check with the ranger station for current road closures. If the roads are open, take some time exploring the area. More material can be found scattered throughout the Hart Mountain area, especially in dry lakebeds and washes. There is beautiful porcelain jasper in the area, but the deposits are very high in the hillsides and even tougher to access. I have found some small float pieces while exploring, but nothing to really report about. Fisher has some GPS readings on his *Ore Rock On* DVD if you're interested in more information on accessing the hard to reach porcelain jasper sites. I have also heard that there is fire opal on Hart Mountain.

74. Crane Creek

Dig for thundereggs in the pits left by previous rockhounds.

See map on page 195.

Land type: Pine forest

County: Lake

GPS: N42 06.168' / W120 15.900', 6,073 ft.

Best season: Late spring–fall

Land manager: BLM—Lakeview

Material: Thundereggs

Tools: Pick, shovel

Vehicle: High-clearance 4WD

Accommodations: Primitive camping throughout BLM land; lodging in Lakeview

Special attractions: Hart Mountain National Antelope Refuge; Hart Mountain Hot Springs; Oregon Outback Scenic Byway

Finding the site: From Lakeview head about 4.5 miles south of town on US 395 (Fremont Highway). Take a left (east) onto Crane Creek Lane. Travel 2.2 miles to a fork in the road. You will cross the creek a few times on this jaunt. Take the fork to the right following the creek until you come to a pullout just before a major washout. Most vehicles cannot make it past this point. If you have very high clearance and 4WD you may be able to make it. Use extreme caution if you do. Continue past the washout from about 0.4 mile to a road leading down the hill and over the creek. Take this road 0.8 mile up the hill to a fork. Take the fork to the left and travel about 0.5 mile to a very steep road leading up the hill to your right. The beds are easily seen about 200 feet up this road.

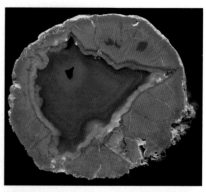

A cut and polished thunderegg from Crane Creek. From the Lantasov collection.
Photo by Yuri Lantasov

Rockhounding

The beds containing thundereggs near Crane Creek are not easily accessible. Part of the road was washed out and only very high clearance 4WD vehicles should even consider attempting crossing the washouts and places where creeks cross the road. My poor little truck took a real beating when I was visiting the site. If you can't make it past the washout, then you are looking at a 3.5-mile roundtrip hike. This really is a site for hardcore thunderegg enthusiasts only.

Luckily if you make the heroic trek back to the beds, the digging in the soft soil is fairly easy. Simple pick and shovel work in the soft soil should reward you with plenty of thundereggs to take home and cut open. Just remember that if you had to walk in, you will have to lug your haul all the way back to your vehicle. A sturdy backpack or a Broll may be a good idea to have for a collecting bag if hiking is your only option. The beds are also nicely shaded. Temperatures can get very high during the summer months in this area.

The eggs here have an agate core that tends toward the clear to blue tones. Some banding can occur. The surrounding rhyolite is a nice dark red/brown color that sets off any blue eggs. Great-quality specimens are very rare. Not all the eggs have agate cores and many that do are fractured. Be sure to dig a fair amount of eggs for better luck in finding a keeper when you cut them back at home.

A special thanks to thunderegg enthusiast, Yuri Lantasov, for supplying me with a beautiful shot of a Crane Creek thunderegg. I filled a five-gallon bucket in hope of getting at least one good cut thunderegg for a photograph. As previously mentioned, the road leading in is pretty rough. Upon leaving the site I was so preoccupied thinking about the nasty drive out that I left my bucket of eggs sitting right by the pits. I was already in Klamath Falls by the time I noticed. If you were the lucky one to find a white Do-it Best Hardware bucket full of eggs, you are welcome. Did any of them turn out?

75. Dry Creek

Large chunks of light-red jasper are common throughout the Dry Creek area.

See map on page 195.

Land type: Forested hillsides

County: Lake

GPS: A: N42 03.007' / W120 35.879', 5,869 ft (opal); B: N42 02.687' / W120 37.493', 5,492 ft. (jasper, black quartz)

Best season: Late spring–fall

Land manager: USFS— Fremont National Forest

Material: Jasper, agate, black quartz, common opal

Tool: Geology pick for prying

Vehicle: Any

Accommodations: Primitive camping near Dog Lake, Drews Reservoir, and throughout BLM land; lodging in Lakeview

Special attractions: Drews Reservoir; Oregon Outback Scenic Byway

Finding the site: From Lakeview head west on OR 140 to Tunnel Hill Road, about 7.4 miles. Turn left (south) on Tunnel Hill. After about 3 miles the road changes to Westside Road. Stay on Westside for another 6 miles. Look for Horseshoe Lane on your right (west). Take this road for another 1.5 miles where it turns into NF 4020. From here travel 5.7 miles to Site A. There is a small pulloff marking the spot. Site B is another 1.9 miles down the road. There is a large pulloff at the top of a hill.

Parked at Dry Creek, Site B. Search the hills for jasper and black quartz.

Rockhounding

This area is productive and easily accessible by most vehicles. It would make a nice day trip if collecting at Juniper Ridge or if the road home takes you back toward Lakeview after collecting sunstones. There is also good camping located nearby at Dog Lake and Drews Reservoir. During my visit in late summer 2012, much of the area had recently been damaged by wildfire. Some trees were even still smoking. Check on conditions during the summer fire season for road closures.

Site A has a lot of white common opal scattered throughout the hillside. Keep an eye out for it when pulling up. There is some agate and red to tan jasper strewn about as well. The hills at this site are somewhat steep, so be sure to be in good physical condition if you decide to do some hiking up or down the hill. Bring plenty of water too, as the summer temperatures can get very high.

Site B is not nearly as steep and there is plenty of room to pull off the road. Lots of brick-red to tan jasper can be found in pretty much any direction at this site. Do some exploring to find larger pieces. Some jasper here can be a bit porous, so be picky if you plan on polishing anything. What I found most interesting at this site was the strange black quartz material. It's almost like raw pieces of black agate, but much more quartz-like. It tumbles well and I would imagine larger pieces could make some interesting cabochons. The quartz too seems to be everywhere.

Nearby Drews Reservoir was once a very productive area, but development and ranch land has blocked access to much of the better collecting sites. The area is know for its agate, obsidian, and petrified wood. When I visited in 2012 I was blocked by a new fence and was only able to find a small handful of obsidian chips in the available BLM land.

76. Mud Ridge

A large fist-size chunk of black obsidian found near Mud Ridge.

Land type: High desert sagebrush
County: Harney
GPS: N43 39.469' / W119 10.714', 4,871 ft.
Best season: Summer
Land manager: BLM—Burns
Material: Obsidian
Tool: Geology pick (for prying)
Vehicle: 4WD suggested
Accommodations: None on site; motels and RV parks in Hines and Burns
Special attraction: Malheur National Wildlife Refuge
Finding the site: Traveling east from Bend or west from Vale, use US 20 to get to Hines. At the truck stop on the west end of town, take NF 47 (Hines Logging Road / Burns-Izee Road) north up the hill. Travel 4.6 miles to a gravel road on your right. If you miss the first one take the second at the country triangle intersection. For the next mile there is obsidian in the ditches. The land is private, but you are allowed to collect from the ditches, which are part of the public road. Find a safe place to park and do some ditch exploring. From the intersection travel another 3.4 miles to a gate and a road on your left. Take this turn and drive another 5 miles

Burns Area

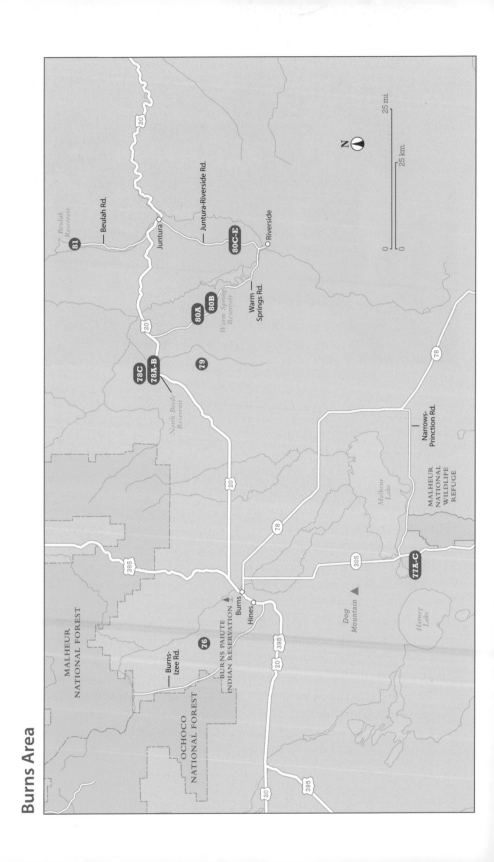

Be prepared to have company while collecting obsidian at Mud Ridge.

down the bumpy washboard road where you will cross a cattle guard. Lots of obsidian will be found along the drive, but most of the land is private, so stick to the ditches here too. Just after the cattle guard a road will lead off to your right. You can follow this road up the hill or park at the bottom to begin your exploring.

Rockhounding

The area north of Hines has long been known for its black, red, and green obsidian. Back in the good ol' days the land was much more open to the public and collecting was great. Unfortunately much of the area is now privately owned and collecting is not welcome. Even more unfortunate is that the area where the green obsidian was known to come from is now peppered with NO TRESPASSING signs. Fortunately, there is still a small plot near Mud Ridge where we rockhounds can still legally collect volcanic glass. Let's make sure to keep it clean and to not over-collect the site, as to keep it available for future generations of rockhounds.

While the quality of obsidian here is generally not as high as the material found at Glass Butte, it is very plentiful. Black is the dominant color. Fist- to double-fist sizes are very common and larger pieces could be found with some searching. If you're lucky you may find some good red obsidian scattered about. Collecting is mostly float hunting. Use a geology pick to help pry pieces out of the ground. If you decide to dig, be absolutely sure to fill in your holes. Remember you're in cattle country, and we want to be on our best rockhounding behavior.

Be warned that the gate to the site is closed in the winter/early spring. Contact the Burns BLM for road closure information. It's absolutely no fun to drive all the way to a destination just to have to turn around and drive home. A quick phone call can save you a lot of trouble.

77. Harney Lake

A double-fist-size chunk of oolitic agate collected at Harney Lake, Site C.

See map on page 202.

Land type: High desert sagebrush

County: Malheur

GPS: A: N43 15.016' / W118 59264', 4,209 ft. (gravel piles); B: N43 14.627' / W118 59.795', 4,246 ft. (gravel piles); C: N43 14.728' / W118 59.659', 4,315 ft. (oolitic agate)

Best season: Spring–fall

Land manager: BLM—Burns

Material: Agate, jasper, petrified wood, oolitic agate

Tool: Geology pick for prying

Vehicle: Any for Sites A and B; 4WD for Site C

Accommodations: RV park at Malheur Lake; primitive camping possible on BLM land; lodging in Burns

Special attractions: Malheur National Wildlife Refuge; Diamond Craters; Crane Hot Springs; High Desert Discovery Scenic Byway; East Steens Tour Route; Steens Loop Tour Route; Diamond Loop Tour Route

Finding the site: From Burns take OR 205 south approximately 24 miles to The Narrows at the southern end of the lakes. Turn left (west) onto S. Harney Lake Road and head 1.5 miles in on this well-maintained gravel road, just past the cattle guard. To your right (north) is a pullout with gravel piles. This is Site A. Back on S.

The view of Harney Lake from Site C is breathtaking.

Harney Lake Road, continue heading west for approximately 0.8 mile to a turnout on your left (east) to reach Site B. A few hundred yards south, in the turnout for Site B, you'll see a road leading up the butte. This leads to the oolitic agate at Site C. It's only about 0.2 mile up the butte, but the hill leading up is very steep and bumpy. Most people would just prefer to hike the short distance.

Rockhounding

This is a great site for rockhounding not only for the abundant material, but also the absolutely beautiful scenery and other recreational activities. Nearby the Malheur National Wildlife Refuge is a seasonal and permanent home to more than 320 bird species and fifty-eight mammal species. There is a well-known eagle's nest perched on the cliffs near Sites B and C.

The gravel piles at Sites A and B are full of highly polished pebbles of agate, jasper, and petrified wood. Collecting is just a matter of walking around and picking them up. Stones here have been ground by Harney Lake and have gained a surprisingly high polish for naturally tumbled stones. It wouldn't take much work to bring these pebbles to a high-gloss polish in a tumbler. The material never seemed to get over a couple of inches in size, but there is so much of it you'll have no trouble filling your collecting bag. Spend some time and search as many gravel piles as you can. The agate and jasper come in many colors and the petrified wood tends to be in gray, black, and brown tones.

Site C is up on top of the hill and boasts an interesting variety of agate called oolitic agate. I can't for the life of me find any information about how it forms, but there were certainly a lot of bubbles involved in some way. Large pieces offer potential for very interesting slabs and cabochons. Do some walking around to find larger chunks and keep an eye out for icebergs poking their heads out of the soil. Also be sure to bring a camera for the spectacular views from on top of the hill. The views of the lake and surrounding area are breathtaking.

78. North Beede Reservoir

An agate stuck in the ground at North Beede Reservoir. Use a geology pick to pry stubborn material out of the cement-like dirt.

See map on page 202.

Land type: High desert sagebrush

County: Harney

GPS: A: N43 45.293' / W118 28.532', 3,686 ft.; B: N43 45.788' / W118 29.317', 3,740 ft. (fossil leaves); C: N43 47.139' / W118 28.984', 3,840 ft.

Best season: Late spring–summer

Land manager: BLM—Burns

Material: Agate, jasper, petrified wood, fossil leaves

Tool: Geology pick

Vehicle: 4WD

Accommodations: Camping allowed on BLM land; primitive camping at Warm Springs Reservoir

Special attractions: North Beede Reservoir; Warm Springs Reservoir

Finding the site: From Burns to the west or Ontario to the east, use US 20 to travel to a northerly turn onto a dirt road between mileposts 166 and 167. Travel this road about 0.2 mile to a fence. Go through the fence making sure to close it behind you. Site A is a general area. Park your vehicle just past the fence at the fork in the road to begin your exploring. There is material scattered about everywhere here. Site B is reached by taking the fork in the road to the left. After about 0.7 mile you will reach a creek. If you have a high-clearance 4WD vehicle you can ford the creek here and continue. If not, your journey is probably at an end. Take it from me; I got stuck in the mud here once. Luckily the fossil leaves are just past the creek in the white cliffs so they are within walking distance if you can't make it past the creek. Site C is found by continuing 1.9 miles along the road from the creek. When you reach a fence, park and begin your hunt.

Rockhounding

The scenic hills around the North Beede Reservoir are littered with agate, jasper, and petrified wood. To top it all off, there is a nice exposure containing fossil leaves. The collecting begins not far from the highway and even though the roads leading into the site are rough, if you have the right vehicle you should have no problems. You must have 4WD and high clearance in order to ford the creek that crosses the road a couple times on the way in. Most vehicles should be able to make it to Site A with little trouble. Sites B and C require a high-clearance vehicle.

At Site A, park and hike the area looking for float agate, jasper, and petri-fied wood. The material is generally tumbler size, but fist-size material can be found now and again. Some of the agate can have a nice blue tint to it, but

Search the sagebrush near North Beede Reservoir for plentiful agate, jasper, and petrified wood.

most is clear to gray. The jasper is generally red to yellow. Petrified wood is found in brown and red tones.

Site B boasts some nice leaf fossils. Bring your geology pick or a hammer and chisel. Split chunks of the chalky material to try to expose a whole leaf or multiple specimens.

The material found at Site C is pretty much the same as what's found at Site A. Site C is a bumpy drive, but the size of material found here tends to be a bit larger than at Site A, making the rough couple of miles worth it. If you have a good rig and a sense of adventure, I highly recommend making it back there. If you can't drive in past the creek, it is possible to hike in. Just be in good physical condition and be sure to bring plenty of water. Don't forget your collecting bag.

79. Stinkingwater

A small, yet very nice piece of Stinkingwater petrified oak.

See map on page 202.

Land type: High desert

County: Harney

GPS: N43 39.964' / W118 28.009', 3,882 ft.

Best season: Late spring–fall

Land manager: Private—open to collecting by custom. Be on your best behavior.

Material: Petrified wood, agate

Tools: Pick, shovel, hammer, gad, geology pick

Vehicle: 4WD

Accommodations: Primitive camping on site; lodging and RV parks in Burns and Hines

Special attraction: Warm Springs Reservoir

Finding the site: From Burns head east on US 20 to just after milepost 167. Turn south onto an unmarked gravel road. This is Stinkingwater Creek Road. Drive about 6 miles to a bumpy dirt road heading west. Drive this road about 0.9 mile to an intersection, turn left, and travel another 0.3 mile to the bottom of a hill where you will meet the creek. You can park and get started here or continue and explore the many spur roads in the area.

The petrified wood collecting area at Stinkingwater.

Rockhounding

Exceptionally beautiful golden-yellow petrified oak has made this locality popular for generations upon generations of Oregon rockhounds. The oak takes a wonderful polish and it is possible to find large pieces. Please take note that I said possible and not likely. The best float was picked up many decades ago. Word is that the BLM filled in big old pits at some point, making it difficult for new rockhounds to locate a good place to get started. I didn't make my first trip here until 2013 and I saw no pits. I even tried to get an old local rockhound to accompany me on my visit to help me find the old pits, but there was no getting him out there.

The big prize here of course is the beautiful golden yellow oak, but there is more wood to be found throughout the area. This is not a site for the faint of heart. The area is very hot and the only way to find good material is by doing a lot of hiking and being very lucky or by digging—and digging deep. The material can be as deep as 4 to 5 feet down, so be prepared to dig a serious hole. Human backhoes need only apply. I did not dig during our visit, but I did find some very nice tumbler material strewn throughout the aromatic sagebrush. If you go about the float collecting way, get away from the road to have a better chance of finding larger material. That being said, I did find a few nice tumbler-worthy pieces in the middle of spur roads, so keep alert no matter where you are in the area.

There is a pleasantly cool and shaded creek running through the site, making a very welcoming oasis in the hot and dusty high desert. Songbirds, dragonflies, hummingbirds, and katydids were all drawn to the water, as well as ground squirrels, little lizards, deer, and watchful hawks. We found a couple of nice camping spots near the site, one on top of the hill before you go down to the creek and the other at the bottom of the hill near the creek, with a very large shade tree and an interesting firepit.

80. Warm Springs Reservoir

Petrified wood, plume agate, and rhyolite collected at various sites around Warm Springs Reservoir.

See map on page 202.

Land type: High desert sagebrush

County: Harney, Malheur

GPS: A: N43 40.369' / W118 20.322', 3,798 ft.; B: N43 38.776' / W118 18.724', 3,586 ft. (dry wash); C: N43 35.641' / W118 09.191', 4,272 ft. (Apache tears); D: N43 36.001' / W118 09.048', 4,197 ft. (stock pond); E: N43 36.403' / W118 09.009', 4,089 ft. (dry wash)

Best season: Late spring–early fall

Land manager: BLM—Burns; BLM—Vale

Material: Chalcedony, agate, moss agate, plume agate, jasper, petrified wood, Apache tears

Tools: Geology pick, shovel

Vehicle: 4WD recommended

Accommodations: Primitive camping at Warm Springs Reservoir

Special attraction: Warm Springs Reservoir

Finding the site: There are two ways to get to the sites at Warm Springs Reservoir. Both are accessed from US 20. Get to the Juntura area using US 20. I'm going to give directions from the westernmost entrance. Look for Warm Springs Reservoir

Road found just east of milepost 171. The road is all gravel and dirt from here on in. Site A is a general area. My GPS marking is simply a good place to get started. Feel free to explore any open dirt road you may find. Drive 8 miles until you find a dirt road shooting off on your right. Take this bumpy road about 0.4 mile to a small parking area by a hill and a gate. Site B is reached by continuing along the main road another 2.8 miles to a pullout just before a cattle guard. Park here and explore the dry wash on the south side of the road. To reach Site C continue along the main road for 7.9 miles to a fork. This is Reservoir Road. Take the fork to the left up the hill and drive another 4.2 miles to another fork where you'll stay to the left onto Juntura-Riverside Road. Travel another 3.6 miles to a pullout on your left. Site C is the dry wash found just south of the pullout. Continue along the road for another 0.5 mile north to reach Site D. You will notice a stock pond to the west. There is no pullout here, so park to the side of the road as much as you can. Search the hills on both sides of the road. Site E is another 0.5 mile north on the road. You will see a dirt road shooting off to the west following a dry wash. Park at the pullout at the beginning of this road or follow it if your rig is sturdy enough. From Site E it is another 13 miles to US 20 in Juntura.

Rockhounding

The area surrounding the Warm Springs Reservoir is rich with agate, jasper, and petrified wood. The sites listed here were found to be very productive, but just about anywhere can be prosperous. Plan to have lots of time for exploring while visiting the area. An ATV would be a great thing to have out here, as there are lots of bumpy roads shooting off from the well-maintained main road. There is a plume agate claim south of the reservoir and I have seen pictures of small fluorite cubes found in the area. The rockhounds who have claimed to have collected fluorite in this area have their lips sealed on its exact location.

Site A has mostly agate and jasper, but some petrified wood can be found. Some of the agate can have moss or plume inclusions. This site is just a recommendation for where you might start exploring the area. You can find material down just about any dirt road on this side of the reservoir. Search the hills for exposures and concentrations of rock. Be sure to have a geology pick to help pry out icebergs, as there are many.

Site B is a dry wash found near a cattle guard and a good pullout. There's more of the same agate and jasper here, but you might also find an interesting sort of bird's-eye rhyolite. Most of the rhyolite is fairly porous, but some pieces are solid and could make for some interesting lapidary work.

Collecting agate and jasper at Warm Springs Reservoir, Site A.

At Site C there are some small mostly opaque Apache tears found in a dry wash and around the hills. They tumble well, that is if you can find enough of them. They are not super plentiful.

Site D has some decent petrified wood. Most of it is not high quality, but a few pieces are highly agatized and take a great polish. All of it has great cellular replacement. The wood ranges from mostly brown to brick-red tones and some can have some agate veins running through it. When I visited it didn't look like many people knew about this spot. I easily found my twenty-five-pound limit in about a half hour and everything I found was float. There were lots of material by the stock pond and throughout the hills on both sides of the road. I imagine that digging would be a fruitful endeavor. Remember to fill in your holes if you decide to dig as this is cattle country. The only drawback to this site is there's no good parking. If you collect here, be sure to pull as far to the side of the main road as you can. Luckily there's not much traffic going through this area.

Site E is another dry wash stretching out to the west. Some good tumbler-size agate and petrified wood can be found easily in the wash and throughout the hills. If you have a sturdy rig or an ATV, you can drive down the dirt road parallel to the dry wash. If not, you can park near the main road and hike the area.

81. Beulah Reservoir

A fossil "helicopter" found by Sally on the shore of Beulah Reservoir.

See map on page 202.

Land type: Reservoir shoreline

County: Malheur

GPS: N43 54.703' / W118 09.504', 3,362 ft.

Best season: Summer

Land manager: BLM—Vale

Material: Leaf fossils, agate

Tools: Geology pick, hammer, chisel, packing materials

Vehicle: 4WD suggested

Accommodations: Primitive camping near reservoir

Special attraction: Beulah Reservoir

Finding the site: Coming from Burns or Ontario, use US 20 until you get to the town of Juntura. Turn north onto Beulah Road and drive down the gravel road for about 15 miles until you get to the reservoir. Take a left and cross the dam. The road will curve to the right just after the dam and a large pullout will be on your right. Park here, backtrack down the hill a bit, and follow the short road down to the reservoir shore and the chalky white deposits.

A view of the mentioned collecting site at Beulah Reservoir Park in the pullout on the ridge above the collecting site.

Rockhounding

Scenic and beautiful Beulah Reservoir is surrounded by chalky white outcrops that happen to be chock-full of excellent leaf fossils. To top it off there are random agates and jaspers to be found about as well. They aren't quite as interesting as the fossils, but they're there and some specimens are big enough to tumble. The scenery is beautiful and despite a 15-mile drive down a gravel road, the site is very easy to find from US 20 in Juntura. There is also good camping throughout the area.

The GPS reading that I took for this site is just one of many places we found fossils on our visit. Sally found a particularly excellent maple seed "helicopter." You can use my reading or explore the reservoir and find your own deposits. Just about any chalky white outcrop has potential. It would be very handy to have a boat to reach otherwise inaccessible areas, and there is a boat launch.

Find a good deposit of chalky white material and start looking for fossil exposures. Some break naturally in neat stacks and are just waiting for you to separate the layers, exposing a stone tablet scrapbook of prehistoric pressings. Others need to be exposed by breaking the material apart and crossing your fingers in hope that it splits in the right spot. Tapping on the up-ended plane of layers works best. It may take you some practice getting the right swing of the hammer, but with some patience you'll have it down in no time. Take your time and hold out for complete fossil specimens or pieces containing multiple species of petrified flora. Be sure to bring packing material for your fossil finds or your fragile specimens may not make it home with you; paper towels, newspaper, and plastic grocery bags are quite suitable.

82. Cottonwood Creek

Agate, jasper, and chert found in the abundant gravels of Cottonwood Creek.

Land type: Creek gravels
County: Malheur
GPS: A: N43 44.417' / W117 40.435', 3,046 ft. (pullout near bridge); B: N43 42.622' / W117 42.177', 3,154 ft. (pullout near tree)
Best season: Late spring–fall
Land manager: BLM—Vale
Material: Jasper, picture jasper, chalcedony, agate, moss agate, Apache tears (obsidian)
Tool: Geology pick
Vehicle: 4WD suggested
Accommodations: Camping allowed on BLM land
Special attraction: Historic Vale
Finding the site: Do not attempt these roads in wet weather. From US 20 (Central Oregon Highway) travel about 20 miles west of Vale. Look for Crowley Road to the south between mileposts 222 and 223. Take Crowley Road and drive south for about 9.4 miles until you reach a small bridge. There is parking on the right just before you cross. This is Site A. Site B is reached by driving another 2.6 miles south on Crowley Road. You will see a road on your right. Take this road about 300 feet and park at the edge of the gravel.

Owyhees

The gravel deposits of Cottonwood Creek stretch on as far as the eye can see.

Rockhounding

The gravel deposits at Cottonwood Creek are absolutely huge. They are wide and stretch on for as far as the eye can see. You could spend days exploring this plentiful rockhounding area. You will find lots of tumbler material as well as a few pieces large enough to slab. Be sure to bring plenty of water and sunscreen, as this area can get very hot and especially dry. Watch out for huge dust clouds created by the occasional vehicle passing by on the dirt road.

Jasper is the most common mineral found in the creek. Much of the jasper is in the brown tones, but you may also find some in tones of yellow, red, and green. I found one little piece that was a bright lime green with some agate running through it. We also found a bit of low-grade, although colorful, picture jasper. I'm confident that with some time and diligent searching, one could find some good hard picture jasper.

The agate isn't quite as common as the jasper. It's mostly clear to light blue in color, but some moss agate can be found as well. I found a nice big chunk that at first just looked like green jasper. The moss inclusion was so tight and thick that the agate was almost opaque. It also had little red splotches similar to bloodstone.

Keep an eye out for Apache tears and chunks of obsidian as well. Some of it is high grade, but a lot of it is junk. Chip off an edge to determine the quality. I didn't find much decent petrified wood during my visits, but I wouldn't be surprised at all if other rockhounds were to find some. The surrounding area is rich with high-quality petrified wood.

83. Skull Springs

I found agates in dry washes a couple miles south of Skull Springs.

See map on page 217.

Land type: High desert sagebrush

County: Malheur

GPS: A: N43 34.750' / W117 43.792', 4,526 ft. (beginning of general obsidian area);
B: N43 27.021' / W117 47.147', 4,262 ft.; C: N43 25.285' / W117 46.007', 4,279 ft.

Best season: Spring–fall

Land manager: BLM—Vale

Material: Apache tears (obsidian), agate, jasper

Tool: Geology pick

Vehicle: 4WD suggested

Accommodations: Camping allowed on BLM land

Special attraction: Historic Vale

Finding the site: From US 20 find Crowley Road between mileposts 224 and 225.
From here on the road can be iffy. Do not attempt in wet weather. Take Crowley
Road south for about 11 miles until you start seeing obsidian on and lining the
road. From here on until about Skull Springs there is obsidian. At 34.1 miles down
Crowley Road is Site B. Site C is just down the road at about 37 miles in.

Searching the gravels of dry washes south of Skull Springs. Please take note that I am not wearing proper footwear for rockhounding, especially in the desert.

Rockhounding

All along Crowley Road heading south from Harper are excellent rockhounding opportunities. Look for obsidian, agate, and jasper just about everywhere you can get legal access. You will pass Cottonwood Creek (Site 82) on your way in, and these sites just add to the expedition. Check out just about everywhere you can find exposed rocks. There is a lot of private land in the area, so bring a good BLM map with you to avoid trespassing if you plan on doing some exploring. When in doubt, a fence means keep out.

Site A is a general area. From about 11 miles down Crowley Road to Skull Springs there are Apache tears just about everywhere. I cannot think of any other place in Oregon where I have seen more. There are also many decent fist-size chunks of obsidian. We found black, lace, and mahogany obsidians, but I wouldn't be surprised if one were to find more varieties of volcanic glass. Basically, find a safe place to pull out and start hunting. Keep an eye out for dry washes and concentrations of shiny black Apache tears.

Sites B and C are just a few miles south of Skull Springs. They are both dry washes that cross the road. Search the wash in either direction of the road for agate and jasper float material. The agate is mostly clear and a lot of it is banded or has nice quartz crystals. The interesting agate here has a red/orange tone and in a lot of ways resembles fire agate found in the southwestern

A couple of oddly shaped agates found in the dry washes south of Skull Springs. The round one on the left is about 3 inches in diameter.

United States. I have not found any "fire" inside these agates, but it sure is similar. It's sort of a fire-less fire agate. The jasper we found here was mostly red to yellow.

There are some thunderegg beds east of Skull Springs, known locally as the Skull Spring Beds, Dry Creek Beds, or Harper Beds. As the crow flies the beds are only a couple miles down a spur road shooting off of Crowley Road. That being said, the spur road leading in is very rocky and proved to be too much for my little Toyota. Fisher has these pits marked on his DVD, if you really want to find them. Keep in mind that the only way you're going to get back there is with a rugged 4WD vehicle or an ATV.

84. Vines Hill

Abundant obsidian Apache tears can be found scattered throughout the Vines Hill area.

See map on page 217.

Land type: High desert

County: Malheur

GPS: A: N43 53.857' / W117 26.681', 2,882 ft. (dirt road); B: N43 54.054' / W117 25.976', 2,885 ft. (highway road cut)

Best season: Any

Land manager: BLM—Vale

Material: Apache tears (obsidian), petrified wood

Tool: Geology pick

Vehicle: Any for Site B; 4WD suggested for Site A

Accommodations: None on site; lodging in Vale

Special attraction: Historic Vale

Finding the site: Site A is located between mileposts 232 and 233 on US 20. Follow the dirt road on the north side of the road for about 0.1 mile or so and find a place to pull out and park. You can also just park at the entrance and walk in. Site B is a small pullout just east of milepost 233. Find a safe place to pull off the highway.

Reaching out for an Apache tear at Vines Hill, Site B. Be sure to pull well off the road when collecting at this site.

Rockhounding

Excellent Apache tears litter the hills west of Vale. They are very abundant and easy to collect. The obsidian looks nice both rough or tumble polished. You should have no trouble finding enough to charge your tumbler. I suppose if you have a twelve-pound tumbler or bigger, it may take you a bit longer to fill it, but it's not impossible. There's also a bit of petrified wood scattered about, but it is much less common than the obsidian.

Site A is just off the highway and a good place to pull off and stretch your legs while traveling. Find a safe place to park and locate the dry wash on the north side of the dirt road. You will immediately begin finding Apache tears and the occasional piece of petrified wood. Follow this dry wash as it heads up the hill.

Site B is a pullout near a road cut and a guardrail right on US 20. Pull off as far from the highway as you can. I would not recommend this site if traveling with small children or pets. I would however recommend it if you're traveling with limited time to rockhound. In just a few short minutes, you should be able to pick up a handful of shiny black Apache tears. Search the ditches and road cut for material.

85. Negro Rock

Search the washes near Negro Rock for tumbler- to fist-size pieces of petrified wood.

See map on page 217.
Land type: High desert
County: Malheur
GPS: N43 41.860' / W117 23.558', 3,176 ft.
Best season: Late spring–fall
Land manager: BLM—Vale
Material: Petrified wood, agate
Tools: Geology pick, pick, shovel
Vehicle: 4WD
Accommodations: Twin Springs Campground; camping allowed on BLM land
Special attractions: Owyhee Reservoir; Thunderegg Coffee Company (Nyssa)
Finding the site: Directions given here are from Nyssa. This way is the least bumpy. The site can also be reached from near Vale using Rock Canyon Road. From Nyssa drive south from town on OR 201 about 8 miles and take a right onto Owyhee Avenue. Drive 6 miles to Mitchel Butte Road and take a left. Drive 0.5 mile to a fork in the road and take it to the right. Drive 4.9 miles to a fork and stay to the right. Drive another 3.6 miles to another fork. Take the road to the far left and drive 6.9 miles to a spur road shooting off past Negro Rock. You can park here and begin your explorations. There is a nice dry wash nearby.

The hills near Negro Rock have high-quality petrified wood. Be prepared to do some digging for the big stuff.

Rockhounding

Some of Oregon's top-shelf petrified wood comes out of the hills of and surrounding the landmark called Negro Rock. (Some of the old maps will list this site with a much more offensive moniker.) This spot has turned out some of the best petrified wood in Oregon for decades. The amazing thing is that you can still find decent float randomly throughout the sagebrush and in dry washes. Be prepared to do some serious hiking for the best material. Have good hiking shoes and bring plenty of water.

The petrified wood found here has excellent cellular replacement and takes one heck of a polish. The color of the wood mostly ranges in the brown, black, and gray tones. You should have no problem finding good tumbler-size material. Bring your lucky rabbit's foot for the big stuff. Use caution and common sense when exploring any spur roads in the area; they can be quite rutted and you're going to be very far away from everything if you get stuck.

Once you have located the site, there are two ways to go about collecting. Like I mentioned, there is still some decent float lying around. Get away from the road for a better shot at finding larger material. The GPS listed here will get you next to a decent dry wash, but after a while this spot will get a bit picked over, so get to exploring. Remember to look under the sagebrush. There could be petrified wood hiding under there.

The second method of attack would be putting a shovel in the ground. This is hard work, especially out here in the hot desert. You're also going to have to be extremely lucky. This is one of those spots where you could dig all day and find nothing. You could also luck out and pull out a nice round log. It's all a roll of the rockhound dice.

86. Twin Springs

A view of Site B, located just a few miles south of the Twin Springs Campground.

See map on page 217.

Land type: High desert

County: Malheur

GPS: A: N43 35.897' / W117 24.322', 3,066 ft.; B: N43 34.819' / W117 24.322', 2,937 ft.

Best season: Spring–fall

Land manager: BLM—Vale

Material: Agate, jasper, basanite, geodes, quartz crystals, petrified wood

Tool: Geology pick

Vehicle: 4WD suggested

Accommodations: Twin Springs Campground; camping allowed on BLM land

Special attractions: Owyhee Reservoir; Snively Hot Spring; Thunderegg Coffee Company

Finding the site: The sites can be reached from either Nyssa or Vale. The route from Nyssa is a bit less bumpy. Either direction is a long dusty drive. From Nyssa, drive south from town on OR 201 about 8 miles and take a right onto Owyhee Avenue. Drive 6 miles to Mitchel Butte Road and take a left. Drive 0.5 mile to a fork in the road and keep to the right. Drive 4.9 miles to a fork and stay to the right again. Drive another 3.6 miles to another fork. Take the road to the left

Our lizard friend back at the Twin Springs Campground, guarding our treasures.

this time and drive about 12.7 miles to the Twin Springs Campground. From the campground continue another 1.2 miles to a dirt road leading to the east. Take this road about 0.2 mile to a dry wash and park your vehicle. This is Site A. Site B is about 2.8 miles from the campground. Find the pullout, which has a geological marker, on your right (west) and park.

Rockhounding

Just a couple miles south of the Twin Springs Campground is an excellent area to rockhound in. Many people come to this campground to rockhound nearby Negro Rock and Haystack Rock. Twin Springs provides yet another place in the area to weigh down your vehicle with more treasures. With delicious, manually pumped spring water and a pit toilet, the campground is a welcome oasis while rockhounding in the desert. It's about the only place in the area where you'll find any shade trees. Two old grave markers fuel imagination and campfire ghost stories. The campground is teeming with abundant wildlife, from large migrating waterbirds to curiously thirsty lizards that will entertain you to the fullest.

The agate is very abundant and sizes range from tons of tumbler material to the occasional piece large enough to cut and slab. Most of the agate found will be clear to light blue in color, much of it with banding. That being said, Sally found a large piece of water-worn agate with orange and red streaks running through it. I almost parked on top of it. A few nodules contain clear quartz crystals. Many of them are just jumbled masses of quartz crystals, but the occasional nice open geode can be obtained. Small loose crystals that have broken out of geodes can be found as well.

My favorite material at this site is the jasper. It's not nearly as common as the agate, but the nice stuff is *really* nice. There's a lot of boring, wannabe jasper everywhere. Hold out for good hard pieces containing good color. The color is generally brown in tone, but some pieces have psychedelic swirls and bands of blue, green, and/or gray running through the brown. It makes excellent lapidary material and produces stunning cabochons. Basanite, or black jasper, is fairly common at Site A and is commonly used for knapping.

While in the area doing research, I high-centered my truck and got stuck as I attempted to turn around on a narrow, nasty road at Haystack Butte— more than 20 miles from camp and about 14 from town. I ended up having to hike 10 miles through the desert with no water (I unwittingly drank it all before I got stuck). A nice young man named Aiden happened upon me and took me the last few miles on his dirt bike. I finally got water and a cell signal and was able to get help. I'm very fortunate to have met kind strangers and good friends in Nyssa. That town is A+ in my book. While Sally was back at camp, wondering what happened to me, she did some hiking on the road for a few miles north of the Twin Springs Campground. There she found even more agate and some nice jasp-agate, so be sure to do some exploring while in the area.

87. Haystack Rock

Wet cut slabs of jasper collected at Haystack Rock. MACALEVY SPECIMEN

See map on page 217.

Land type: High desert

County: Malheur

GPS: N43 42.890' / W117 14.720', 3,066 ft.

Best season: Late spring–early fall

Land manager: BLM—Vale

Material: Petrified wood

Tools: Pick, shovel, geology pick, hammer, chisel, gad

Vehicle: 4WD suggested

Accommodations: Twin Springs Campground; camping allowed on BLM land

Special attractions: Owyhee Reservoir; Thunderegg Coffee Company (Nyssa)

Finding the site: From Nyssa, drive south from town on OR 201 about 8 miles and take a right onto Owyhee Avenue. Drive 6 miles to Mitchel Butte Road and take a left. Drive 0.5 mile to a fork in the road and take it to the right. Drive 4.9 miles to a fork and stay to the left. Continue another 2.5 miles down the hill to a dirt road on your left. You can park here or along this road and start exploring. The GPS taken was way up the steep and rugged road. If your vehicle can handle this road, be my guest. The GPS marking was taken about 1.2 miles up this nasty track.

Northwest Diehard Rockhounds Kaisey Macalevy, Nate Macalevy, and Tony Funk checking out the view at Haystack Rock. Photo by Tammie J. Macalevy

Rockhounding

Haystack Rock is one of many first-rate rockhounding opportunities in the Owyhee area. Excellent jasp-agate, agates, and jaspers can be found at the site itself and also in the surrounding hills, ravines, and gullies. I've never found any in this particular spot myself, but I wouldn't be surprised if some agates and jaspers turned up, and maybe some petrified wood too. Make sure you have plenty of time on your hands to explore this vast collecting area. I've been back here several times and still feel like I've only scratched the surface.

When you arrive at the site, you have a couple of options for collecting. If you have a high-clearance 4WD, you can make your way up to the top of the hill and dig in pits left behind by others. If your vehicle isn't rugged enough, you can park at the bottom of the hill and hike up, or you can hike around the area searching dry washes and ravines. Search for colorful agates, many of which are fist size or bigger. The jasper can come in just about any color as well. The jasp-agate found here takes a great polish and makes for some very nice cabochons.

Be very careful when exploring any spur roads in the area. Twice, while researching for this book, I got adventurous and got myself high centered down dusty and steeply rutted roads. These life-threatening experiences made for two very long, hot, and stressful days. Luckily, I know wonderful people in the area who were willing to drive deep into the desert to rescue me and my truck. Spur roads should only be explored by very high clearance, well-outfitted, rugged 4WD monsters with experienced drivers. Also be sure to have plenty of, if not too much, water and sunblock on hand. This part of the state always seems to be consistently hotter than the rest of Oregon whenever I check the weather.

88. Leslie Gulch

Look for a variety of colorful jaspers in the gravels of the Owyhee Reservoir shoreline.

See map on page 217.

Land type: Reservoir shoreline

County: Malheur

GPS: N43 19.348' / W117 19.562', 2,711 ft.

Best season: Spring–fall

Land manager: BLM—Vale

Material: Jasper, picture jasper, moss agate, agate

Tool: Geology pick

Vehicle: 4WD suggested

Accommodations: Camping in Leslie Gulch

Special attractions: Leslie Gulch, Succor Creek Natural Area; Echo Rock Hot Spring, Thunderegg Coffee Company (Nyssa)

Finding the site: From US 95 take Succor Creek Road north for 9.9 miles. Follow the sign and turn west onto Leslie Gulch. The gravels are found after about 14.3 miles at the end of the road. Park where you can find a safe pullout at the shore. Leslie Gulch can also be reached from OR 201 (S. Adrian Boulevard) between Adrian and Homedale. Take Succor Creek Road south 25.7 miles to the Leslie Gulch turn.

Low water levels at the Owyhee Reservoir give rockhounds more gravels to choose from, with better access.

Rockhounding

Leslie Gulch is arguably one of Oregon's most scenic drives and hiking destinations. The erosion-carved ash deposits are absolutely breathtaking and the mind can run wild with the many shapes. Be sure to bring a camera, as you'll want to remember this area forever. To top it all off, at the end of the drive is the Owyhee Reservoir, which has huge gravel deposits full of excellent lapidary material that can keep just about any rockhound busy all day. This is one of those sites favorable to watercraft. Exploring the many gravels of the Owyhee Reservoir with a raft or boat would be a blast.

The jasper is plentiful and comes in just about every color. Most of it is very hard and will take an excellent polish. It will be a lot shinier than the rest of the rocks lying about and easy to spot. There is a lot of low-grade picture jasper, so hold out for good pieces with lots of silica. Sometimes chipping off a small piece on the corner of suspect material will tell you of its quality. The rind can be deceiving.

Keep your eyes peeled for moss agate. It's not very common, but it's there. I found a nice-size piece with red spots. It looks like a sort of translucent bloodstone. Small bits of clear to light blue agate can be found as well, but with the other excellent lapidary material available, you'll hardly even notice it.

I have an old map I got from the Nyssa Chamber of Commerce that shows some quartz crystals along the drive in. They're somewhere near Juniper Gulch, but the map isn't very specific and I was unable to locate any good quartz. Also on the drive in, before you get to Leslie Gulch you will notice a spur road leading off to the north. It's marked by a sign with petrified wood collecting rules. We drove down the road a bit, but didn't find anything. I'm sure there's something out there or else there wouldn't be a sign. I know there is some picture jasper way back down the road, but most of the sites are under claim.

89. Rockville

A small selection of agate, jasper, petrified wood, and rhyolite found near Rockville.

See map on page 217.

Land type: High desert

County: Malheur

GPS: N43 19.373' / W117 07.225', 3,842 ft.

Best season: Late spring–early fall

Land manager: BLM—Vale

Material: Petrified wood, agate, jasper

Tools: Geology pick, pick, shovel

Vehicle: 4WD

Accommodations: Primitive camping in and around Succor Creek State Park

Special attractions: Succor Creek State Park; Leslie Gulch

Finding the site: From the Succor Creek Recreation Area, drive south on Succor Creek Road. About 1.1 miles south of the turn for Leslie Gulch, you will reach the town of Rockville. Take the dirt road heading west and head up the hill. Drive until you basically can't anymore (less than 0.5 mile) and begin exploring. You can also easily reach this site from US 95 south of Rockville using Succor Creek Road.

A view of the white hills near Rockville. All of these hills have good collecting opportunities.

Rockhounding

Just south of Succor Creek, the white hills near the town of Rockville are full of mostly low-quality opalized wood. The material can get pretty big however, and can be fairly stable if it has not been exposed to the elements for long. The occasional piece of hard agatized wood can be found as well. The petrified wood found here is very similar to what is found at Succor Creek, Site C. Agate is fairly common as well and is found in clear, blue, and iron-stained tones. There is also some very nice banded rhyolite that tumbles well.

After you locate the white hills and park your vehicle, plan on doing some hiking in the hills to find bigger and better material. Search around for small float material and partially exposed logs. If you start finding bits and pieces of wood at the bottom of a hill, move your way uphill to locate what it is breaking off of. Also look out for pits and holes where people have been digging previously. This is strong evidence that something was worth digging out and that there may be more to find.

Bring a good collecting bag, plenty of water, and sunscreen. This area can get especially hot and blistering in the summer. I got burned pretty badly on the back of my neck and elbows while researching the area. Wear good thick gloves if you plan on digging. The opalized wood can splinter and get you good, just like real wood. I caught a nice piece right under a fingernail. Please learn from my mistakes.

90. Succor Creek

A cut and polished Succor Creek thunderegg. RICE NORTHWEST MUSEUM OF ROCKS AND MINERALS SPECIMEN

See map on page 217.

Land type: High desert

County: Malheur

GPS: A: N43 29.986' / W117 07.967', 2,646 ft. (creek gravels); B: N43 27.229' / W117 07.088', 3,041 ft. (thundereggs); C: N43 23.603' / W117 07.759', 3,705 ft. (Round Mountain); D: N43 23.302' / W117 07.759', 3,679 ft. (dry wash)

Best season: Summer

Land manager: Sites A, C and D: BLM—Vale; Site B: Oregon Parks and Recreation

Material: Agate, picture jasper, thundereggs, plant fossils

Tools: Geology pick, hammer, gad, pick, shovel

Vehicle: 4WD

Accommodations: Primitive camping throughout BLM land and along Succor Creek

Special attractions: Leslie Gulch; Owyhee Reservoir; Thunderegg Coffee Company (Nyssa)

Finding the site: From Nyssa or Homedale take OR 201 to Succor Creek Road and head south. Site A is about 11.9 miles in. Find a place to park by Succor Creek Road or take one of the spurs heading to the east to gain access to the creek. Site B is

A far-off view of the campground and thunderegg beds at Succor Creek.

another 3.6 miles south on Succor Creek Road. Park at the campground and cross the footbridge to reach the site. Site C is about 5.7 miles south of the campground. Park in the pullout. Grass Mountain is to the east. Site D is another 0.5 mile from Site C where you'll find another pullout. You'll see the dry wash from here. These sites are also accessible from US 95. Take Succor Creek Road north and drive 13.6 miles to Site D.

Rockhounding

Simply put; Succor Creek is awesome. Not only is there a wide variety of fine silicate materials available for digging, but the area is full of stunning vistas and geological interests. Do not forget your camera when visiting this wonderful part of the world. You'll never forgive yourself if you do. People have been digging rocks and fossils in the Succor Creek area for many years, and scientists first began studying the fossils found here in the 1920s. Luckily there is still plenty of material to collect. The sites listed here are just some good places to start. Be adventurous and do some exploring on your own.

At Sites A and D you'll be searching the creek gravel deposits. At Site A, the better deposits are across the creek. Find a safe place to cross and don't forget your mucking shoes. Cross the creek and search for agate, jasper, picture jasper, and petrified wood. You will also find material in the dry washes to the west of here.

Crossing Succor Creek a few miles north of the campground. There's a great big gravel deposit over there.

Site B is located within the park and has a huge thunderegg bed just across the creek from the campground. Cross the footbridge and you'll immediately begin to notice paths running up the hill. These lead to places where people have been working material out of the hard rhyolite matrix. If you don't have hard-rock tools, or just don't feel like the heavy work, search the talus all around the base for loose eggs. Search the hill to both the north and south for eggs. This is also a good area to hike around Succor Creek for gravel deposits.

Site C is a petrified wood deposit found on Round Mountain in a layer just above the ash deposit. It's quite a hike up the hill to find the deposit. Most of the wood is opalized and crumbly. Some harder pieces can be found with diligent searching. For those who don't want to hike, some float wood, jasper, and agate can be found in the dry washes around the area.

If your travels happen to take you through the city of Nyssa (the Thunderegg Capital of the World), be sure to make a stop at the Thunderegg Coffee Company at 125 Main Street. The owners are very friendly, especially to this rockhound who got chased out of nearby Homedale, Idaho, by some especially unfriendly locals. The cafe also happens to make a great cup of coffee and sandwiches. They have lots of local thundereggs on display to check out while you wait. Tell 'em Lars says hi.

91. Graveyard Point

A lichen-encrusted piece of Graveyard Point plume agate.

Land type: High desert sagebrush
County: Malheur, Owyhee
GPS: A: N43 34.466' / W117 01.250', 2,471 ft. (Graveyard Point marker); B: N43 33.217' / W117 02.835', 2,593 ft. (beginning of collecting area); C: N43 32.861' / W117 03.156', 2,686 ft. (intersection); D: N43 32.465' / W117 02.900', 2,772 ft.; E: N43 32.632' / W117 03.283', 2,840 ft. (big pit); F: N43 32.406' / W117 03.063', 2,815 ft. (small pits)
Best season: Spring–late fall
Land manager: BLM—Vale
Material: Plume agate, agate, basanite
Tools: Geology pick, hammer, gad, chisel, pry bar
Vehicle: 4WD suggested
Accommodations: Primitive camping on site and throughout BLM land; Snake River RV park located in Homedale, Idaho
Special attractions: Owyhee Uplands Back Country Byway; Western Heritage Historic Byway; Jump Creek Waterfall; Thunderegg Coffee Company (Nyssa)
Finding the site: To reach this site you will need to go through Idaho. From where Main Street in Homedale, Idaho, junctions with US 95, head south on US

Graveyard Point

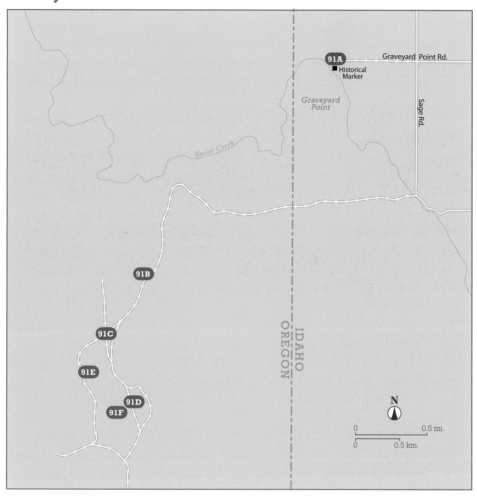

95 for 3 miles. Take a right (west) onto Graveyard Point Road and travel 3.9 miles to the junction at Sage Road. To get to Site A, continue forward on Graveyard Point Road for 0.2 mile to the historical marker and collection area. To get to Sites B–E, take a left (south) on Sage Road and head 0.9 mile to a dirt road with a small bridge on your right (west). Take this road and follow it to the left and avoid the private homes to your right. There should be a sign that says BLM and has an arrow pointing you in the right direction. From here on in the dirt roads get very rutted. A couple hundred feet past the bridge you will take a right. Drive about 2.6 miles

due east, where you will reach Site B. From here you continue on for 0.5 mile to reach an intersection, and Site C. Go left at the intersection toward Site D. Drive 0.2 mile to a fork and stay to the right, Site D will be on your left in about 0.1 mile. To reach Sites E-F from the (Site C) intersection, head up the hill (SW) 0.4 mile to a parking area on your left and Site E. From here, Site F is reached by continuing along the road for 0.4 mile to a turn on your left. Head up to the top of the hill and look for pits.

Rockhounding

Areas like Graveyard Point are why people say that Oregon is where rock-hounds go to die. Though it has been a popular rockhounding destination for decades, you can still find plenty of agate just lying around waiting for you to dig or pick it up. There are tons of float, ranging from tumbler-size material to chunks you could cut small slabs from. Large slabable pieces can be worked out of seams in the surrounding hillsides. There's so much agate you should have no problem collecting abundant specimens. I've literally had to slap myself on the wrist to stop myself from bringing home "too much material." Keep in mind that there are many claims in the area. They are usually marked by PVC pipes or wooden posts.

The prized material here is the plume agate, displaying a wispy feather-like inclusion in white, pink, and black tones. There is also moss, dendritic, orange, blue, polka-dot, tube, banded, and countless other varieties of agate to be found as well. If you love agate you'll never want to leave this site. My GPS markers are just a few places you can achieve success. This is a vast area and there are many places to find great material. Some exploring should reward you handsomely.

Site A is actually in Idaho and has been a popular collecting area for many generations; great material can still be found. Collecting at this site is somewhat limited due to private land and a canal that is not easy to cross. This is however about the only site that a passenger car can make it to. If you don't have a sturdy rig, Site A is about your only chance for collecting. All rockhounds should make an effort to visit the historical marker at least once.

Site B is located along the road leading in. This is the beginning of the general collecting area. Park in the large parking area and search the hillsides for agate. There is also some basanite found in this area. I found some petrified wood nearby, but I have suspicions that it is from somewhere else. I found it

Early morning at Graveyard Point. It's best to beat the heat when collecting here.

fairly close to where someone was obviously high-grading their material. I could be wrong, so keep your eyes peeled.

Site C is an intersection where you can park and head in almost any direction. I would suggest wandering far off into the hillsides to search for material. Lots of moss agate and dendritic agate can be found here. Make sure to have a strong collecting bag if you plan to hike. You will find material and you will have to drag it all the way back to where you parked.

Site D is a small hill where you can find some small, but good-quality white plume agate veins. There's decent float material to be found, but if you want bigger pieces you'll have to locate a vein and do some hard-rock mining.

Site E is a series of large pits left from a past plume claim. This site is a hard-rock mining operation. There are some very large veins exposed just waiting to be worked. Bring your tools to get some big pieces. You can also find float by hiking up the hill.

Site F marks a bunch of small pits on top of a hill. There is more plume agate and other agates found here. Pick a pit to expand on, or start one of your own.

92. Rome

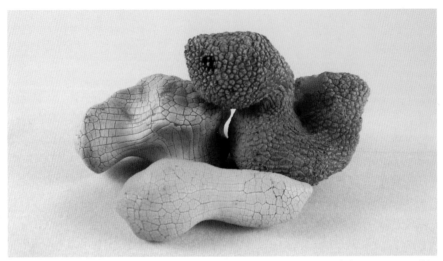

Snakeskin agates collected near Rome. The eye on the "Oregon duck," as people have come to call it, is natural.

Land type: High desert sagebrush
County: Malheur
GPS: A: N42 47.172' / W117 44.175', 3,661 ft. (Apache tears); B: N42 46.087' / W117 44.108', 3,676 ft. (common opal); C: N42 45.551' / W117 43.690', 3,737 ft. (snakeskin); D: N42 45.551' / W117 43.895', 3,744 ft. (snakeskin)
Best season: Summer
Land manager: Private—open by custom to casual collecting. Be on your best rockhounding behavior. If you come across "keep out" signs or fences, then respect the owner's rights and stay out.
Material: Snakeskin agate, Apache tears obsidian, jasper, petrified wood
Tools: Geology pick, shovel, screen
Vehicle: 4WD
Accommodations: Primitive camping near site
Special attractions: Pillars of Rome; Jean Baptiste Charbonneau Gravesite
Finding the site: Head west from the town of Rome on US 95. Just after milepost 59 take the dirt road on your left due south. The cattle guard at the entrance is in bad shape. Be careful crossing it. There used to be a tall sandstone pillar that made

Southeast

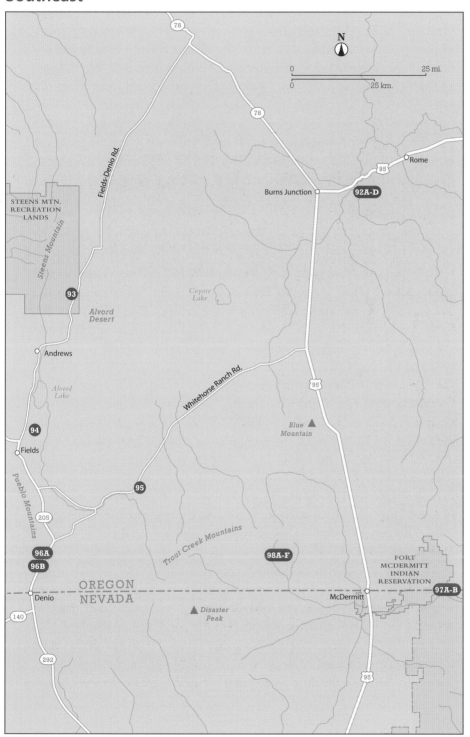

finding this area easier, but it has fallen down in recent years and is now just a pile of rubble. Follow the dirt road as it veers to the left. After 1 mile turn right. This is when the road starts getting really rough with deep ruts everywhere. Head 0.8 mile until you begin to see pebbles scattered throughout the hills. This is Site A and is where obsidian, jasper, and petrified wood can be found. Head another 0.6 mile and take the road on your left. The road will be easy in some spots and rutted in others. Take it slow. After 0.5 mile you'll come to a wash that has more obsidian to collect. Another 0.5 mile down the road you'll find Site B, where the green common opal can be found. Continue about 0.8 mile farther down the road to a fork. To the left is Site C about 0.4 mile in. To the right is Site D at about 0.7 mile.

Rockhounding

Rome is one of my favorite places to dig. It's nestled in one of the most remote parts of Oregon and is the perfect spot to get away from it all. The terrain here resembles what the moon might look like with sagebrush. The only reminder of the world out there is the occasional sound of semi trucks' compression brakes on the highway just a few miles away. I rarely see other rockhounds when I dig here, probably because this site is not on the way to much of anything. Snakeskin agates are the only reason I make it to this part of Oregon.

The road leading away from the highway gets progressively worse the farther you drive in. Don't leave the highway unless you truly believe in your vehicle and are well stocked with supplies. While the digging area is just a couple miles from US 95, this really is one of the most remote areas in all of Oregon.

Once you finally drive all the way out here and pass the bumpy dirt road, the collecting is plentiful. The first collecting opportunity at Site A boasts some decent Apache tears. Walk around and collect yourself a tumbler load, as the material tumbles well. You will also find agate, jasper, and petrified wood scattered throughout the hills. There are more Apache tears in the wash about 0.5 mile from Site B.

Site B is a hill littered with dark green common opal. Most of it has a porous white crust. The green opal inside looks like it might take an okay polish.

Snakeskin agate gets its name from the rough snakeskin-like surface displayed in fine specimens. The crust can be white, gray, rust-orange, black/blue, or a combination of all. I prefer the agates rough, but some people like to tumble polish specimens to exaggerate the snakeskin pattern. The agate itself can come in colors including white, colorless, yellow-green, or bluish, and can

A perfect example of what not to do in Rome. Please fill in your holes folks.

contain inclusions. They are, for the most part, just lying there waiting for you to pick them up. Bring a geology pick to stir up the soil and help pop them out. There are many icebergs, revealing only a small portion above the surface. Some of the largest agates I've found here were showing only a dime-size orb. Another good method for finding big agates is digging and screening. Take precautions and keep yourself hydrated if you plan on doing some shovel work, as it can get very hot at this location.

Site C is just past a dry wash that some vehicles may not be able to make it over. If not just park and walk the short rest of the way. Look for snakeskin agates on the ground or locate the large mess of pits people have left behind. Please fill in your pits if you decide to dig. If cows start getting injured out here, there is a good chance this site could get shut down. Pack out what you pack in as well.

Site D is similar to Site C. Find a good place to pull off the road and begin your hunt for either float or evidence of pits. If you go the digging route, you can either continue where someone was digging previously, or you may start a pit of your own.

93. Pike Creek

A beautiful Pike Creek thunderegg specimen, sliced in half. MACALEVY SPECIMEN

See map on page 243.

Land type: High desert sagebrush

County: Harney

GPS: N42 34.585' / W118 31.847', 4,318 ft.

Best season: Spring–fall

Land manager: BLM—Burns

Material: Jasper, agates, moss agate, thundereggs

Tool: Geology pick

Vehicle: 4WD

Accommodations: Camping on site; fee camping at Alvord Hot Springs

Special attractions: Alvord Desert; Alvord Hot Springs; High Desert Discovery Scenic Byway; East Steens Tour Route; Steens Loop Tour Route; Diamond Loop Tour Route

Finding the site: From Burns, take OR 78 (Steens Highway) south for 64.6 miles to Folly Farm Road/Fields-Denio Road. Take a right and continue for 39.1 miles to a rough dirt spur on your right. You can park at the bottom of this road, or if you have a very rugged vehicle you can drive all the way to the end, a bit over a mile in. The campground is about halfway up this road.

A view of the collecting area at Pike Creek.

Rockhounding

The eastern slopes of the Steens Mountains are well known by collectors for their beautiful thundereggs. Even with the known deposits, thundereggs from this site are not seen very often. Two reasons exist. First, there are few roads that can easily access the thunderegg beds. Secondly, the thunderegg deposits all mostly lie within wilderness boundary, and even if you could drive right up to a deposit, you are not allowed to dig on wilderness land. You can however surface collect and Pike Creek has the only access by road these days.

Pike Creek flows out of the Steens Mountains and into the Alvord Desert. There is a nice camping area along the creek with trees and big boulders for shade. The creek itself is usually running all year. Explore the creek bed, hills, and up the canyon for thundereggs. There also is an old uranium mine about a mile up the creek from the camping area. I have been to this site twice now, yet have only found bits of agate and a couple nodules of what I believe are thunderegg cores. That being said, my friends who come here a lot always seem to walk away with at least a couple of decent saw-worthy eggs and some moss agate. It can be sort of hit or miss in these hills.

If you happen to find yourself getting skunked in this area, you can always go a few miles south and check out Borax Lake (Site 94). There are no thundereggs at Borax Lake, but you won't find yourself leaving empty handed. The

Moss agate found at Pike Creek. MACALEVY SPECIMEN

Alvord Desert is a beautiful place to visit in Oregon. You can drive out onto the playa and head across the desert. Fisher reports an agate deposit across the desert at Tule Springs on his DVD. The one time I tried, I couldn't find it. There are also reports of a sunstone deposit off to the east, but it is claimed, and from what I'm told, very difficult to access anyway. We can only hope someone may open a fee dig out there someday.

There is a fee hot spring just south of the Pike Creek site. It is on private property (Alvord Ranch) and until recently was free to the public. Years of upkeep has pushed the ranch owners into charging a small fee for use of the spring. They also have a fee day use/camping area.

94. Borax Lake

A small sample of agate, jasper, obsidian, and zeolite collected at Borax Lake.

See map on page 243.

Land type: High desert sagebrush

County: Harney

GPS: N42 18.772' / W118 37.238', 4,087 ft.

Best season: Late spring–fall

Land manager: BLM—Burns

Material: Apache tears (obsidian), agate, jasper, petrified wood, zeolites

Tool: Geology pick

Vehicle: 4WD

Accommodations: Camping allowed on BLM land; primitive camping at Pike Creek, fee camping at Alvord Hot Spring

Special attractions: Alvord Desert; Alvord Hot Spring; Steens Mountains; milk shakes at Fields Station in Fields

Finding the site: At the junction of OR 205 and Fields-Denio Road, you will notice a power station and a dirt road shooting off to the east following the power lines. The road is washboard most of the way and I wouldn't recommend it in wet weather. Take this road 2.1 miles to a dirt road on your left (north). From here on in you will find material. I found a good pullout 1.1 miles up this road. We explored the area until reaching the fences about 2.2 miles in and found material the whole way.

After collecting at Borax Lake and having a milk shake in Fields, I highly suggest taking a walk with a loved one over the Alvord Desert playa.

Rockhounding

The area surrounding Borax Lake in the Alvord Desert is littered with Apache tears, agate, jasper, and zeolites. Although everything found here is pretty small, there are lots of materials worth picking up to feed your tumbler. This is also a good place to stop if you find yourself getting skunked at nearby Pike Creek. Be sure to double up on water and your sunscreen, as the Alvord Desert is extremely hot with services few and far between.

Look for dry washes with lots of exposed rocks. Bring a geology pick or some other tool to help pry stubborn pieces out of the cement-like ground. The small black Apache tears are the most common material found here. The agate is generally clear with some banding. There are many small pieces of broken geodes that would be suitable for wire wrapping. The jasper is generally brown or red and the zeolites are white and fibrous.

There are some hot springs surrounding Borax Lake. They're not the nice take a dip in kind, but the burn you badly, scalding kind. There are signs and fences surrounding the springs and hotpots. Be sure to keep a sharp eye on any small children or pets if you decide to rockhound near the hot pools. If you want to take a dip, I suggest going to the Alvord Hot Springs north of Borax Lake. They used to be free to visit, but there is now a small fee for 24-hour access.

After a long hot day of collecting, I highly suggest making it down to Fields and getting a delicious milk shake at Fields Station. They are absolutely refreshing on a hot day and they have a large selection of flavors to choose from. My favorite flavor is chocolate-banana. Fields Station is also about the only place around to get supplies if you're camping in the area. I found they have an excellent beer selection, especially for a small town. Cheers.

95. Chalk Canyon

Search the white hills near Chalk Canyon for abundant leaf fossils.

See map on page 243.

Land type: High desert

County: Harney

GPS: N42 11.948' / W118 20.453', 4,797 ft.

Best season: Late spring–fall

Land manager: BLM—Burns

Material: Fossil leaves

Tools: Geology pick, hammer, chisel, packing materials

Vehicle: 4WD suggested

Accommodations: None on site; camping at Willow Creek Hot Spring

Special attractions: Willow Creek Hot Spring; Alvord Desert; Fields Station (milk shakes in Fields)

Finding the site: The site can be reached from both US 95 and OR 205 (Fields-Denio Road). From OR 205 drive 8.2 miles south of Fields. Turn east onto Whitehorse Ranch Road and drive 14.5 miles to a dirt road leading to some white cliffs in the distance. From US 95 take Whitehorse Ranch Road about 32.7 miles to the same dirt road. Take the dirt road and travel about 0.3 mile to a fork in the road, bear to the left, and continue 0.2 mile till you reach a fence. Travel through the fence, making sure to close it behind you, and drive to the base of the white cliffs.

Fresh fossil-bearing matrix can be worked out of the outcrop found high up on the hill at the collecting site.

Rockhounding

Excellent specimens of leaf fossils from the Trout Creek Formation can be obtained from the chalky white cliffs found near Flagstaff Butte in the aptly named Chalk Canyon. The GPS waypoint I took was at a very productive and easy to reach spot. Just about anywhere you see an accessible white chalky exposure, which is public land, stop and check for fossils.

Once you have located a good chalky exposure, start cracking open chunks of the white material. It may take you some practice and patience to get the right swing of the hammer down, but once you do get it you should start finding more leaf fossils than you will know what to do with. There are a couple of ways in which you can find chunks for breaking open. You can either break open talus material that has weathered out of the hill, or you can hike your way up to the top and work out fresh material. However you choose to find fossils, be very picky and hold out for good whole leaves and specimens containing multiple species of fossil flora. Wrap your fragile finds in paper towels to protect them on the bumpy ride home.

My favorite part of the area was the Willow Creek Hot Spring. Sally and I visited this site after spending 4 days exploring the vastness that is McDermitt. Needless to say we were extremely dirty and desperately needed a good washing; we affectionately call hot springs "rockhound bathtubs." There is an excellent campground located at the springs with a pit toilet. The hot spring has two pools: one is fairly hot and very clear, while the other is warm and slightly silty. Also if you happen to find yourself traveling through the town of Fields, be sure to get yourself a nice cold milk shake at Fields Station.

96. Pueblo Mountains

A small sample of epidote, galena, and quartz found at the Pueblo Mountains, Site A.

See map on page 243.

Land type: High desert

County: Harney

GPS: A: N42 04.098' / W118 36.458', 4,378 ft.; B: N42 02.699' / W118 37.084', 4,348 ft.

Best season: Late spring–fall

Land manager: BLM—Burns

Material: Quartz, epidote, serpentine, galena, schist, copper ores

Tools: Geology pick, hammer, shovel

Vehicle: 4WD

Accommodations: Camping allowed on BLM land; camping at Alvord Desert

Special attractions: Alvord Desert; Steens Mountains; milk shakes at Fields Station in Fields

Finding the site: From Fields, head south on OR 205 for almost 16 miles until you see a dirt road shooting off to the west. The Colony Ranch will be to the east at this point. Take the dirt road for 0.3 mile until you get to a pullout just before a hill. Site B is another 1.4 miles south on OR 205. Look for another dirt road heading to the west. Drive about 0.4 mile to the end of the road and park.

Search the hills of the Pueblo Mountains for abundant quartz, epidote, galena, and copper ores.

Rockhounding

The 170- to 200-million-year-old volcanic hills of the Pueblo Mountains south of Fields offer rockhounds a terrific opportunity for collecting a plethora of material. Big chunks of white quartz, bright green epidote, green serpentine, sparkly schist, metallic galena, and brilliant copper ores are just some of the many minerals to be found in this once explosive area. Now that the volcanos have stopped erupting, we rockhounds can go harvest the mineralogical fruit.

To find most of the mineral in this area, you just have to walk around and pick it up off the ground—that is if you can. Some of the pieces of quartz we found were absolutely huge. They would be great for garden rock, but you'll definitely need a very good friend to help you lug them back to your vehicle. For galena and the copper ores, you're most likely going to have to bust open some rock. Bring a good heavy hammer if you are interested in collecting ores. We did find some nice galena naturally exposed on one piece, but it was just the one. Be prepared to do some hiking to find bigger and better material.

There are some old abandoned mines up Arizona Creek north of Site A. Unfortunately it is about a 2-mile hike in, and this area of the state gets awfully hot. When we visited the area it was 98 degrees, and I wasn't about to even consider a 4-mile roundtrip hike, especially having to lug rocks on the way back. No thank you, ma'am. Instead we opted for milk shakes in Fields at Fields Station.

97. McDermitt East

Thundereggs litter the ground at this hard to reach McDermitt thunderegg locality.

See map on page 243.

Land type: High desert

County: Malheur

GPS: A: N45 11.985' / W117 31.516', 4,938 ft. (creek gravels; Nevada); B: N42 00.089' / W117 29.836', 5,288 ft.; C: N42 00.244' / W117 29.716', 5,301 ft.

Best season: Late spring–fall

Land manager: BLM—Vale

Material: Thundereggs, jasper, agate

Tools: Geology pick, pick, shovel

Vehicle: 4WD

Accommodations: Camping allowed on BLM land

Special attraction: Historic McDermitt, Nevada

Finding the site: Do not attempt these rough roads in wet weather. You'll also have to ford a creek twice along the way. To reach the sites take US 95 about 2.5 miles south of McDermitt, Nevada. Take N Road 5.0 miles through the Fort McDermitt Reservation to an intersection. Take a right and travel 1.7 miles to where the pavement ends and NF 083 begins. Site A is 5.4 miles in from here. To reach the thunderegg beds in Oregon, take this curvy dirt road 7.1 miles in beginning at NF 083 to a steep road on your left. Take this road about 0.2 mile up the hill and back into Oregon to a fork in the road. Site B is located at the fork. Take the fork to the right to find Site C just a few hundred yards down the road on your right.

Don't forget to bring your favorite bucket or two to this remote thunderegg locality. You didn't drive all the way out here for nothing, did you? Fill that thing up!

Rockhounding

The hills east of McDermitt are littered with a wide variety of thundereggs. They sometimes roll down the hill and can be found in the creek gravels as well. The beds have been under claim in the past, but as of 2013 no claims were held. If you find current claim markers, please respect the claim holder's rights and restrict your collecting to areas not claimed, float collecting, or collecting in the creek gravels. There are other thunderegg beds located in Nevada, but I only included the sites found in Oregon and just barely at that. You'll be collecting right on the state line.

Site A is actually in Nevada, but is along the drive in and is a good place to find great material. Just before the creek crosses the road, there is a good pullout. Park here and begin your exploration. Both broken and whole thundereggs can be found in the gravels along with colorful jasper and agate. Some of the agates are actually thunderegg cores freed from their rhyolite shells. You'll also find some thundereggs in the road cut a short distance from the creek, but most are duds containing no agate.

Sites B and C have float thundereggs lying about everywhere. They are generally small (1–2 inches) but larger specimens can be found with diligent searching and some digging. At Site B someone has exposed the actual thunderegg bed itself. You can bust out fresh eggs here with hammers, chisels, and gads. The rhyolite shells come in an array of colors including brown, red, green, and black. The agate inside is even more varied in color and inclusions. Banding, crystals, moss, and plumes can all be found. There are even more eggs located up the very steep hill beyond Site B. If you have a hardcore vehicle or an ATV, you may want to do some exploring in these productive hills. Be very observant of the boundaries between reservation land and BLM land, as this is a sensitive issue among the locals, and trespassing is not tolerated.

98. McDermitt West

A sample of McDermitt minerals found at the sites listed in this book.

Land type: High desert

County: Malheur

GPS: A: N42 03.768' / W117 56.159', 5,676 ft. (purple agate); B: N42 03.731' / W117 56.789', 5,610 ft. (White Hill); C: N42 03.544' / W117 57.989', 5,493 ft. (agate nodules and thundereggs); D: N42 03.751' / W117 57.805', 5,549 ft. (gopher holes); E: N42 04.156' / W117 58.016', 5,616 ft. (Serena green jasper); F: N42 04.390' / W117 57.942', 5,705 ft. (bog agate)

Best season: Late spring–fall

Land manager: BLM—Vale

Material: Petrified wood, agate, jasper, opal, thundereggs

Tools: Geology pick, shovel, pick

Vehicle: 4WD

Accommodations: Camping allowed throughout area; lodging and RV park in McDermitt

Special attraction: Historic McDermitt

Finding the site: Do not travel these roads in wet weather. Using US 95, travel to McDermitt, located on the border of Nevada and Oregon. Take Cordero Mine Road west for 4.3 miles to Disaster Peak Road, a gravel road on the right. Drive 7.4 miles down Disaster Peak to a turn on your right (Archie Myers Ranch Road). Take the right and head down the hill 0.2 mile to a nice place to camp. Mark your odometer from where you cross the creek. The turn for Site A is 2.3 miles down the road and about 1.5 miles up the hill. GPS will really help with this site. Site B is 0.3 mile past the turn for Site A and hard to miss. It's a huge white hill. The turn for Site C is on your left another 1.2 miles from Site B. Drive to the end of this short road until you reach a fence and park. The "gopher holes" area begins another 0.1 mile down the main road from the turnout for Site C. There are a couple pullouts along the road on your right. The turn for Sites E and F is about another 0.2 mile from the "gopher holes" on the right (north). Site E is about 0.3 mile up this road. Site F is about another 0.2 mile farther up. There will be another spur road on your right worth exploring.

Rockhounding

The hills around McDermitt, Nevada, are a rockhound's dream come true. The minerals found in many shapes and forms have kept miners, both professional and amateur, coming to these hills for decades. Energy companies to this day are still exploring and testing the mineral-rich area for resources. There are claims held all over by both rockhounds and big business. Keep your eyes peeled for markers.

The sites listed here are just a small sample of what can be found in the area. I've spent a fair amount of time in McDermitt over the years and still feel like I've only just scratched the surface. Fisher has done a great job documenting many of the pits found around McDermitt. Consult his DVD for more information. Be adventurous and do some exploring on your own. You never know what you'll stumble upon.

Site A has some interesting purple agate. It is usually found as a thin botryoidal crust on the hard host rhyolite. With some luck and some searching, good pieces with lapidary value can be obtained. On your drive in from the main road, watch for agate and petrified wood.

Site B is known as White Hill. It's a big white hill that people have been pulling large petrified wood logs out of for decades. There's still some good wood left, but you're going to have to work for it. Look where others have been digging and try your luck. If you can't find anything big, walk around and collect some good tumbler material. Old timers tell me that some fossil fish have been found in one of the smaller mounds on the west side of the big hill.

McDermitt West

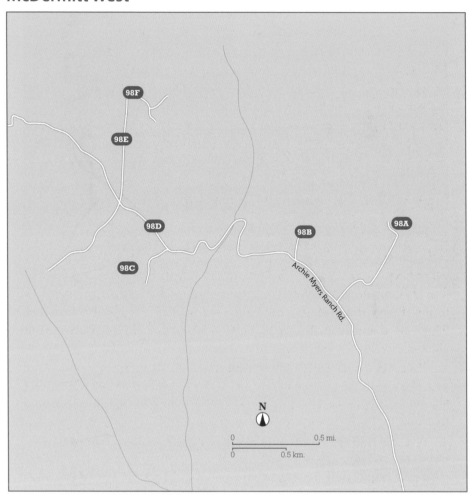

Site C has some agate nodules and jasper that are great for tumbling. There's also a thunderegg bed located at this spot. I've had a few old timers tell me I'm crazy, but it's there. The eggs are found in a hard perlite layer a few hundred feet below the parking area and near the fence. The egg bed needs a few thousand more years of erosion, or a very determined rockhound, as the eggs are not easy to extract. It's not easy to locate either, but there are a couple places where people have tried digging, so look for their surface scratches.

Bring a detailed map and do some exploring down spur roads in the McDermitt area. You never know what you might find.

Site D is full of petrified wood and is known as the "gopher holes." Other people say it looks like the area got carpet bombed. Rockhounds have been carving out this area for a long time and for good reason. Try your luck in finding excellent specimens and lapidary material.

Site E is an area with a type of jasper known as Serena green jasper. It's absolutely beautiful and takes an excellent polish. Walk the hills searching for float.

Site F is just up the hill from Site E and is full of huge bog agates, bog wood, and some petrified wood. Some of the agates up here are ridiculously huge and quite often have equally huge ant colonies underneath them. A bright green translucent common opal can be found scattered about or attached to agate as well.

APPENDIX A: GLOSSARY

Adit: An entrance to an underground mine.

Agate: A type of microcrystalline quartz exhibiting a pattern or inclusions such as banding, moss, or plumes. Clear "agates" are technically chalcedony.

Ammonite: An extinct type of mollusk closely related to the modern day nautilus.

Amygdule: A hollow space in igneous rock left by gas bubbles during formation. This cavity can then be filled by secondary minerals such as quartz, chalcedony, agate, calcite, and zeolites.

Apache Tear: Small round nodules of obsidian that are generally translucent.

Azurite: A deep blue copper carbonate hydroxide, formed in the oxidized portions of copper deposits.

Banded Agate: Agates with multiple layers of alternating colors.

Basalt: The most common igneous rock on Earth's surface.

Botryoidal: A mineral habit exhibiting a bubbly or globular external form resembling a bunch of grapes.

Brecciated: A descriptive term used for minerals that have broken apart and then later sealed back together by a secondary mineral.

Cabochon: A gemstone that is cut and polished with a domed upper surface and a flat or domed undersurface.

Calcite: A type of calcium carbonate.

Carnelian: A red to orange translucent variety of chalcedony, which is usually colored by iron oxides.

Cellular replacement: When a mineral such as quartz replaces organic materials such as wood.

Chalcedony: A type of microcrystalline quartz without banding or inclusions. Clear chalcedony nodules found on Oregon shores are commonly referred to as "beach agates."

Chalcopyrite: A copper iron sulfide generally brassy in color.

Concretion: A round mineral mass formed in sedimentary rock. Concretions often contain marine fossils that they form around.

Dendrites: A tree-like habit mineral inclusion usually formed by manganese or iron oxides.

Enhydro: A term used for minerals that have water bubble(s) trapped inside of them.

Epidote: A calcium aluminum iron silicate hydroxide generally found in a light to dark green color.

Fee Dig: Pay to play rockhounding. Sites that are privately owned or claimed that charge by weight of material, time, and/or usage.

Feldspar: A group of aluminosilicate minerals. The most common mineral found in the Earth's crust.

Float: Refers to mineral collected on the surface of the ground.

Fortification banding: A type of banded agate with sharp angular corners, much resembling a fort.

Fossil: Any evidence of past life preserved in rock, including bones, shells, footprints, excrement, and borings.

Garnet: An abundant silicate mineral found in metamorphic rock.

Geode: A hollow cavity within rock that is lined with crystals.

Granite: The most common intrusive rock in Earth's crust. The three main minerals it is made up of are feldspar, quartz, and mica.

Habit: The characteristic crystal form or combination of forms of a mineral.

Iceberg: Term used by rockhounds for a specimen that on the surface only reveals a portion of its true size.

Inclusions: A crystal, mineral, or fragment of another substance enclosed in crystals or rock.

Jasper: A variety of opaque microcrystalline quartz.

Lapidary: The craft of shaping stones, minerals, or gems into decorative items such as cabochons, faceted stones, carvings, etc. Also the term used for the craftsperson.

Marble: A granular metamorphic rock derived from limestone or dolomite.

Matrix: The rock or sediment in which a mineral, gemstone, or fossil is embedded.

Micromount: A term used by collectors to describe mineral specimens that are best appreciated using an optical aid, such as a hand-lens.

Moss agate: A variety of agate with moss-like inclusions, usually formed by chlorite or manganese oxides.

Obsidian: A natural volcanic glass formed when lava cools too quickly to form crystal minerals.

Opal: A type of hydrated amorphous silica.

Outcrop: Part of a geologic structure that shows itself on the surface of the Earth.

Overburden: Loose overhanging dirt and rock that overlies a mineral deposit and must be removed.

Permineralized: Material of organic origin that has been fossilized through precipitation of dissolved minerals in the interstices of hard tissue.

Petrified wood: Ancient wood that has had its cells completely replaced by silica, turning it into agate, jasper, or opal.

Pit: A hole that rockhounds dig in.

Plume agate: A variety of agate with feathery plume-like inclusions usually formed by chlorite or manganese oxides.

Pyrite: A brassy colored iron-sulfide. Also known as "fools gold."

Pyroclastic: Rock material formed by volcanic explosion or aerial expulsion from a volcanic vent.

Quartz: A mineral made out of silicon dioxide with a hexagonal crystal structure.

Rhyolite: A relatively rare igneous rock, rhyolite is considered the volcanic equivalent of granite.

Sard: A type of microocrystaline quartz similar to carnelian but generally darker and more brown toned.

Tailings: Piles of rock waste left by gold mining operations.

Tumble: To round and polish a mineral in a mechanical rotary or vibratory tumbler.

Tumbler: A motor-powered device that is used to round and polish hard minerals. They come in rotary and vibratory varieties.

Vug: An open cavity in a rock that will often contain crystals.

Wash: An eroded area of soil caused by occasional running water.

Zeolite: A large family of hydrous calcium, aluminum, or sodium silicate minerals. It is usually formed as an alteration product of igneous rocks.

APPENDIX B: CLUBS

Clubs are a great way to meet other rockhounding enthusiasts. Many offer classes in lapidary skills and host field trips all over the state. Some even have their own claims where only club members can dig. I highly suggest you join one today. All clubs listed were accurate at the time of publication. Please refer to the Northwest Federation of Mineralogical Societies website for up-to-date information on most clubs.

Northwest Federation of Mineralogical Societies
www.amfed.org/nfms/ClubsOR.asp

Astoria
Trails End Gem and Mineral Club
92232 Lewis & Clark Rd.
Astoria, OR 97103
Meetings: Second Mon, 7 p.m.

Central Point
Roxy Ann Gem and Mineral Society
2002 Scenic Ave.
Central Point, OR 97502
(541) 664-6081
www.craterrock.com/roxy-ann-gem-mineral-society
Meetings: Second Fri (except for July and Dec), 7:30 p.m.

Coos Bay
Far West Lapidary and Gem Society
PO Box 251
Coos Bay, OR 97420
Meetings: First and third Thurs, 7 p.m.
Faith Lutheran Church, North Bend

Corbett

Columbia Gorge Rockhounds
15523 NE 215th Ave.
Brush Prairie, WA 98606
Meetings: Third Fri, 7:30 p.m.
Firemans' Recreation Hall
Corbet

Eugene

Eugene Mineral Club
PO Box 26327
Eugene, OR 97402
www.eugenemineralclub.com
Meetings: Third Thurs (except July, Aug, Sept), 7:30 p.m.

Florence

Siuslaw Gem and Mineral Club
PO Box 935
Florence, OR 97439
Meetings: Second Tues, 6:30 p.m.
Siuslaw Valley Christian Center, 10th and Maple

Forest Grove

Tualatin Valley Gem Club
PO Box 641
Forest Grove, OR 97116
Meetings: Second Wed, 7:30 p.m.
Forest Grove Senior Center, 2037 Douglas

Grants Pass

Rogue Gem and Geology Club
PO Box 1224
Grants Pass, OR 97526
Meetings: First Wed, 7:30 p.m.
Fruitdale Grange, 1440 Parkdale Dr.

Gresham

Mount Hood Rock Club
15523 NE 215th Ave.
Brush Prairie, WA 98606
www.mthoodrockclub.com
Meetings: Second Tues and fourth Mon, 7 p.m.
Gresham United Methodist Church, 620 NW 8th St., Gresham

Hermiston

Hatrockhounds Gem and Mineral Society
PO Box 1122
Hermiston, OR 97838
www.hatrockhounds.org
Meetings: Second Tues, 7 p.m.
First Christian Church, 775 W Highland

Hillsboro

North American Research Group
www.narg-online.com
Meetings: First Wed, 7 p.m.
Rice Northwest Museum, 26385 NW Groveland

Klamath Falls

Rock and Arrowhead Club
PO Box 1803
Klamath Falls, OR 97601
www.klamathrockclub.org
Meetings: Second Mon, 7 p.m.
Klamath County Museum, 1451 Main St.

Lakeview

Tall Man Rock Chippers
PO Box 563
Lakeview, OR 97630
Meetings: Second Thurs, 7:30 p.m.
Lake County Chamber of Commerce, 126 N.E. Street

Lebanon
Sweet Home Rock and Mineral Society
PO Box 2279
Lebanon, OR 97355
Meetings: Second Wed (except Aug), 6:30 p.m.
Santiam Place, 139 Main St.

Lincoln City
North Lincoln Agate Society
1423 NW Hwy. 101
Lincoln City, OR 97367
Meetings: Second Tues, 6:30 p.m.
Rock Your World: Pacific NW Gem and Art Gallery, 1423 NW US101

Myrtle Creek
South Douglas Gem and Mineral Club
PO Box 814
Myrtle Creek, OR 97457
Meetings: Second Mon, 6 p.m.
2459 Stewart Parkway Conf. #2, Roseburg

Newport
Oregon Coast Agate Club
PO Box 293
Newport, OR 97365
www.coastagates.org
Meetings: Second Tues, 7 p.m.
Central Lincoln PUD, 2129 North Coast Hwy.

North Bend
Lower Umpqua Gem and Lapidary Society
69833 Stage Rd.
North Bend, OR 97459
Meetings: Second Tues, 2 p.m.
Winchester Bay Community Center, Winchester

Ontario

Malheur County Rock and Gem Club
PO Box 961
Ontario, OR 97914
Meetings: Second Tues, 6 p.m.
Malheur County Extension Office, 710 SW 5th

Oregon City

Clackamette Mineral and Gem Society
PO Box 903
Oregon City, OR 97045
www.clackamettegem.org
Meetings: Third Tues (except July), 7 p.m.
Zion Lutheran Church, 720 N Jefferson St.

Pendleton

Oregon Trail Gem and Mineral Society
1330 SW 39th
Pendleton, OR 97801
Meetings: Third Mon, 7:45 p.m.
Oxford Suites, 2400 SW Court Pl.

Portland

Columbia-Willamette Faceters Guild
PO Box 2136
Portland, OR 97208
www.facetersguild.com
Meetings: First Tues, 7:30 p.m.
1945 SE Water Ave.

Geological Society of the Oregon Country
PO Box 907
Portland, OR 97207
Meetings: Second Fri (Except March, Aug, and Sept), 8 p.m.
Portland State University, Cramer Hall, Room S-17

Oregon Agate and Mineral Society
4821 Grant St.
Portland, OR 97215
www.oregonagate.org
Meetings: First and third Fri, 7:30 p.m.
Powelhurst Baptist Church, 3435 SE 112th

Roseburg
Umpqua Gem and Mineral Society
PO Box 1264
Roseburg, OR 97470
Meetings: Second Mon, 7 p.m.
Community Education Bldg., 2459 Stewart Parkway

Salem
Willamette Agate and Mineral Society
PO Box 13041
Salem, OR 97309
www.wamsi.org
Meetings: First Thurs, 6:30 p.m.
Salem Senior Center, 2615 Portland Rd. NE

Springfield
Springfield Thunderegg Rock Club
PO Box 312
Springfield, OR 97477
www.thundereggrockclub.blogspot.com
Meetings: Second Tues, 7 p.m.
Willama Lane Adult Activity Center, 215 West C St.

APPENDIX C: MUSEUMS

Here are some places where you can go see amazing collections of gems, minerals, rocks, and fossils, and some mining history. Gold brought a lot of people to Oregon, and there are some world-class collections to be found in this great state.

Baker City
Baker Heritage Museum
2480 Grove St.
Baker City, OR 97814
(541) 523-9308
www.bakerheritagemuseum.com

Central Point
Crater Rock Museum
2002 Scenic Ave.
Central Point, OR 97502
(541) 664-6081

Corvallis
College of Earth, Ocean, and Atmospheric Sciences
Oregon State University
104 CEOAS Administration Bldg.
Corvallis, OR 97331-5503
http://ceoas.oregonstate.edu/minerals/

Cottage Grove
Bohemia Gold Mining Museum
737 E Main St.
Cottage Grove, OR 97424
(541) 942-5022

The Dalles

The Columbia Gorge Discovery Center
5000 Discovery Dr.
The Dalles, OR 97058
(541) 296-8600
www.gorgediscovery.org

Eugene

University of Oregon Museum of Natural and Cultural History
1680 E 15th Ave.
Eugene, OR 97401
(541) 346-3024
http://natural-history.uoregon.edu

Fossil

Fossil Museum
Washington and Main St.
Fossil, OR 97830
(541) 763-4481

Oregon Paleolands Institute
333 W 4th St.
Fossil, OR 97830
(541) 763-4480
www.paleolands.org/

Haines

Eastern Oregon Museum
610 3rd Street
Haines, OR 97833
(541) 856-3233

Hillsboro

Rice Northwest Museum of Rocks and Minerals
26385 NW Groveland Dr.
Hillsboro, OR 97124
(503) 647-2418
www.ricenorthwestmuseum.org

Kerby

Kerbyville Museum
24195 Redwood Hwy.
Kerby, OR 97531
(541) 592-5252

Kimberly

Thomas Condon Paleontology Center
32651 Hwy. 19
Kimberly, OR 97848
(541) 987-2333 x0
www.nps.gov/joda/photosmultimedia/Thomas-Condon-Paleontology-Center.htm

Parkdale

Hutson Museum
4967 Baseline Dr.
Parkdale, OR
(541) 352-6808

Portland

Oregon Museum of Science and Industry
1945 SE Water Ave.
Portland, OR 97214
(503) 797-4000
www.omsi.edu

Sunny Valley

Applegate Trail Interpretive Center Museum
500 Sunny Valley Loop
Sunny Valley, OR 97497
(888) 411-1846
(541) 472-8545
www.rogueweb.com/interpretive

APPENDIX D: ROCK SHOPS

Support your local rock shop! Rock shops are not only great places to buy your favorite gems, minerals, and lapidary equipment locally, but quite often the owners and employees can share some local rockhounding information or even provide you with some maps.

Adrian
Steven Jewell Concepts
Stone Delight
707 1st St. (Hwy. 201)
Adrian, OR 97901
(541) 372-0185
(541) 372-3782

Aloha
Sticks in Stones Lapidary
8918 SW Grabhorn Rd.
Aloha, OR 97007
www.sticks-in-stones.com

Ashland
Flower of Life Crystals
40 N Main St.
Ashland, OR 97520
(541) 552-0170
www.floweroflifecrystals.com

Bandon
Jailhouse Rocks
570 2nd St. SW
Bandon, OR 97411
(541) 347-7625

Beaverton
Earthly Treasures
19500 SE Alexander St.
Beaverton, OR 97006
(503) 848-3383

Burns
Highland Rock and Gem
1316 Hines Blvd.
Burns, OR 97720
(541) 573-5119

Central Point
Crater Rock Museum and Gift Shop
2002 Scenic Ave.
Central Point, OR 97502
(541) 664-6081
www.craterrock.com

Corvallis
Al & Merle's Rock and Gem Shop
28816 Hwy. 34
Corvallis, OR 97333
(541) 752-5085

Neukomm Rock and Gem Gallery
2295 NW 9th St.
Corvallis, OR 97333
www.neukommrockandgem.com

Dayville
The Southfork Gem Shop
345 South Fork Rd.
Dayville, OR 97825
(541) 987-2835

Estacada
Mossy Rock
398 Broadway St.
Estacada, OR 97023
(503) 630-3199

Eugene
5 Elements Gem and Mineral
2100 W Broadway
Eugene, OR 97402
(541) 343-2201
www.5erockshop.com

I Love Rocks
1495 Oak St.
Eugene OR 97401
(541) 285-4635

Nelson the Rocky-Feller
1509 W. 6th Ave.
Eugene, OR 97402
(541) 687-8100

Gleneden Beach
The Crystal Wizard
7150 Gleneden Beach Loop
Gleneden Beach, OR 97388
(541) 764-7550

Hillsboro
Rice Northwest Museum of Rocks
and Minerals
26385 NW Groveland Dr.
Hillsboro, OR 97124
(503) 647-2418
www.ricenorthwestmuseum.org

Kerby
Hampton's Rock Shop
194 Finch Rd.
Kerby, OR 97531
(541) 592-2800

Klamath Falls
Dorgene's Rock Shop
4737 Alva Ave.
Klamath Falls, OR 97603
(541) 850-0325

Lakeside
Usrey's Rock Bin
72445 US 101
Lakeside, OR 97449
(541) 759-2321
www.usreysrockbin.com

Lincoln City
Rock Your World: Pacific NW Gem
and Art Gallery
1423 US 101
Lincoln City, OR 97367
(541) 351-8423

Philomath
Get Your Rocks Off
1203 Main St.
Philomath, OR 97370
(541) 936-1715

Plush
Weee Rock
28228 Hogback Rd.
Plush, OR 97637
(541) 947-5913

Portland
Ed's House of Gems
7712 NE Sandy Blvd.
Portland, OR 97213
(503) 284-8990
www.edshouseofgems.com

The Fossil Cartel
1440 Pioneer Place
340 SW Morrison
Portland, OR 97204
(503) 228-6998
www.fossilcartel.com

The Gold Door
1434 SE 37th Ave.
Portland, OR 97214
(503) 232-6069
www.thegolddoor.com

The Third Eye
3950 SE Hawthorne Blvd.
Portland, OR 97214
(503) 323-3393
www.thirdeyeshoppe.com

Prineville
Quants Rock Shop
1411 NE Spruce Lane
Prineville, OR 97754
(541) 447-5548

Redmond
Canutt's Gems
7840 South Highway 97
Redmond, OR 97756
(541) 548-2333

Petersen Rock Garden and Museum
7930 Southwest 77th St.
Redmond, OR 97756
(541) 382-5574

Seaside
Shamouses Rock
1000 Holladay St. #1
Seaside, OR 97138
(503) 539-1290

Selma
Crystal Kelidoscope
18435 US 199
Selma, OR 97538
(541) 597-4300

Shady Cove
Shady Cove Rock and Gift Shop
22074 Hwy. 62
Shady Cove, OR 97539
(541) 878-3433

Silverton

I've Got Rocks in My Head
110 N Water St.
Silverton, OR 97381
(503) 409-4706
www.ivegotrocksinmyhead.com

Tierra Del Mar

Pier Avenue Rock Shop
5845 Pier Ave.
Tierra Del Mar, OR 97135
(503) 965-6334
www.pieraverockshop.com

Vancouver

Handley Rock and Jewelry Supply
6160 Hwy. 99
Vancouver, WA 98665
(360) 693-1034
www.handleyrockandjewelry.com

Yachats

Planet Yachats
281 US 101
Yachats, OR 97498
(541) 547-4410
www.planetyachats.net

BIBLIOGRAPHY

Alt, David D., and Donald W. Hyndman. *Roadside Geology of Oregon*. Missoula, MT: Mountain Press Publishing, 1978.

Daniels, Frank J., and Richard D. Dayvault. *Ancient Forests: A Closer Look at Fossil Wood*. Grand Junction, CO: Western Colorado Publishing Co., 2006.

Drake, H. C. *Northwest Gem Trails*. Portland, OR: Mineralogist Publishing Company, 1950.

Fisher, Tim. *Ore Rock On*. DVD, version 5.2, 2011.

Gladwell, Jon. *A Family Field Collecting Guide for Northwest Oregon and Southwest Washington*, Vol. I, II, III. Portland, OR: Myrddin Emrys Ltd., 2012.

Litton, Evie, *Hiking Hot Springs in the Pacific Northwest*, Guilford, CT: FalconGuides/Globe Pequot Press, 2001.

Mitchell, James R. *Gem Trails of Oregon*, Second Edition. Baldwin Park, CA: Gem Guide Books, 1998.

Myers, K. T., and Richard L. Petrovic. *Agates of the Oregon Coast*. Newport, OR: FACETS Publication, 2008.

Newman, Renée. *Exotic Gems*. Los Angeles: International Jewelry Publications, 2010.

The Ore Bin, Vol. 15, No. 10, October 1953.

The Ore Bin, Vol. 30, No. 4, April 1968.

The Ore Bin, Vol. 31, No. 6, June 1969.

Pabian, Roger K, with Jackson, Brian, Tandy, Peter, and Cromartie, John. *Agates Treasures of the Earth*, Buffalo, NY: Firefly Books (US) Inc., 2006.

Romaine, Garret. *Gem Trails of Oregon*, Second Edition. Baldwin Park, CA: Gem Guide Books, 2008.

Tschernich, Rudy. *Zeolites of the World*. Phoenix, AZ: Geoscience Press, Inc., 1992.

SITE INDEX